THIS BOOK BELONGS TO

The Library of

....

....

Did you like my book? I pondered it severely before releasing this book. Although the response has been overwhelming, it is always pleasing to see, read or hear a new comment. Thank you for reading this and I would love to hear your honest opinion about it. Furthermore, many people are searching for a unique book, and your feedback will help me gather the right books for my reading audience.

Thanks!

Table of Contents

Introduction

Congratulations on purchasing *This Book,* and thank you for doing so. Many people don't understand themselves when it comes to emotions and downloading this book confirms your urge to understand the underlying principles, theories, and unique ways on how to tackle various emotions. Emotion is a complicated and twisted topic, but this book will comprehensively cover all the necessary information you need to learn how to control your emotions. The first chapters define and expound different available emotions and how you can detect a similar emotion.

To the middle and the end of the book, you will learn more about vivid symptoms depicted by individuals who suffer from these emotions as well as their positive and negative impacts on your life. Here, you need to have a reflective reading mode and an open mind to search yourself and determine which emotion is affecting you and whether it is useful or destructive.

The book will illustrate various types of emotions alongside theories about them. You will learn about how you can manage your emotions and how to understand when a particular emotion is extreme. By the end of the book, you will have a clear insight into general emotions, related health disorders, how to manage, and when to know you are suffering from a specific emotion.

There are thousands of similar books, but your decision to download this particular book cannot be taken for granted. Multiple efforts have been utilized to ensure that you get all the information you need. Please enjoy!!

Chapter 1: Introduction to Emotions

In our day to day activities, our actions are mostly advised by different feelings that range from extreme joy to extreme sadness. Human emotion is derived from accumulated feelings that result in an emotional state of being. The emotion involves physiological arousal, and psychological appraisal usually followed by cognitive processes that now inform behavior and action. The emotional state is subjective to experiences, background, culture, and expressive behavior that develops during life and mostly related to childhood interactions between an individual and his or her environment.

Human beings differ in emotional reactions, even in similar circumstances. There is a psychology that gives the human being able to produce and recognize emotional facial expressions without hearing a word from the other individual. Over the years, research on emotion has increased significantly with various fields contributing to and explaining the human emotion. Under these fields, different theories have been created include; Psychology, neuroscience, endocrinology, medicine, history, sociology of emotions and computer science. Even with the multiple fields coming from different schools of thought, emotions define our existence.

Ten Basic Emotions

Basic emotions came about in response to the ecological challenges, with each feeling corresponding to a distinct and dedicated neurological circuit. Just from being hardwired, basic emotions are innate and universal, automatic, and fast often triggered to provide survival value. The underlying feeling is not the same as a complex emotion that highly varies from individual to individual; this type of opinion cannot be attributed to infants and animals. It is because it is a compilation of basic emotions and mostly a blend of basic ones. Primary emotions are generally compared to programs, and they can be open to cultural conditioning. Here are some of the basic emotions that apply in our lives.

- **Sadness:** This primary emotion is categorized under negative emotion. It is often seen as the opposite of happiness even though that does not necessarily apply in every situation or circumstance. Being that it is a single emotion, sadness can be either loss or failure invoked or a psychological response depending on the subject. Sadness is, therefore, characterized by multiple feelings, such as helplessness, despair, loss, grief, and disappointment.
- **Excitement:** Being excited has been termed as 'pure emotion.' This is because it is a feeling or situation usually full of activity, joy, exhilaration or even disruption. The emotion is termed pure since it has no definite goal object. With excitement, there is no definite reaction too. What is sure though, is that the feeling causes activity since a person feels something should be done.
- **Anger:** It is usually an intense emotional state that is mostly associated with response to an action or even a thought. It could involve a strong uncomfortable and hostile response to provocation, hurt, or threat. Someone experiencing anger will also have physical effects on an individual, such as increased heart rate, spiked blood pressure. It is predominant feeling behaviorally, cognitively, and physiologically.
- **Fear:** It is an emotion often caused by the threat of danger, pain, or harm. With fear, the danger is not imminent and is not directed towards an object or situation presenting real danger. The reaction that is fear is involuntary, even when it seems unreasonable. In most

cases, an individual or animal will experience fear of either the known or unknown either through the imagination of experience.

- *Joy:* The feeling of extreme delight, gladness, well-being, or satisfaction is often described as joy. The emotion of joy is not necessarily advised by something positive happening; rather, it could be the exultation of the spirit arising and simply an attitude of the heart or spirit. It is a generalized feeling that comes from deep down.
- *Surprise:* Surprise can be both a negative or positive emotion. It involves a sense usually inflicted by a different party other than you, and either astonishment, wonder, or amazement is usually the response one is most likely to emit. Usually, it is an unexpected emotion and could be sudden depending on the circumstance. Surprise has the power of unlocking other emotions such as anger, joy or even fear.
- *Contempt:* Contempt is an emotion usually acquired when you look down on others, and mostly it involves the judgment of secondary parties and could easily be based on culture, standards, morals, class, and even in some instances, another person's religion might trigger the emotion of contempt. The other person is usually perceived as being less in a way the person feeling contempt considers important. Eventually, the person experiencing contempt creates a relational distance between themselves and the party or parties involved. This way, the emotion brings with it pleasure and superiority to the person feeling it.
- *Guilt:* Feeling regretful, responsible for an offense either in existence or non-existence. During this time, a person believes that they have compromised their own standards or have violated moral standards they had earlier set for themselves. It is a cognitive experience that is closely

related to feeling sorry or remorseful. Guilt could either be a feeling of lacking to do something or doing something an individual is not supposed to do. The emotion of guilt can also be anticipated and avoided in some instances.

- ***Shame:*** The emotion of shame often termed as a moral or social feeling that is discrete and could force an individual to hide or deny action or deed that causes the emotion. Driven by conscience, this is an emotion that breeds an affective state where one experiences conflict at having done something that one believes or is made to believe they should not do and vice versa. The negative effects of the emotion could be withdrawal motivations, feelings of distress, powerlessness, worthlessness, and mistrust.
- ***Disgust:*** This emotion is under negative feelings and a sensation referring to something revolting and could be offending in away. The emotion is associated with aversion or disapproval and is often followed by a sickening feeling of loathing or nausea. The environment around or experience could cause disgust and may be followed by physical expressions, wrinkled nose, narrowed eyes, lowered eyebrows among other muscle reflexes depending on the situation at hand.

Theories of Emotions

Emotions are complex and subjective and often followed by biological and behavioral changes. How we think, feel, or respond to a situation is not predictable, and this is why persons and institutions have invested in trying to explain and understanding emotion. These theories exist as guides giving insights on how to handle certain situations and circumstances. Here are some of these theories;

James-Lange Theory

This theory dates back to 1884 and 1885, and American and Danish psychologists William James and Carl Lange came up with theories on the connection between emotion and physiology. James's research paid attention to emotion as a consequence of physiological change, as Lange emphasized that emotion is a demonstration of physiological change. Together, they combined their theories and combined their names to resulting to the James-Lange theory that seeks to prove that emotions are separable from physiological reactions to events. Initially, the two worked their own theories before combining them.

"Emotion is equivalent to the range of physiological arousal contributed by external events." Explains the theory. "For someone to feel emotion, they must first experience responses from the body, such as increased heart rate, spiking blood pressure as well as respiration." Continues the theory. Based on this physiological arousal, then the person can say that they feel an emotion. This goes beyond the human believe that emotions trigger physiological reactions like; To reinforce their argument, James and Lange say that the automatic activity and actions inspired by emotional stimuli generate feelings of emotion and not vice versa. This means that if you hear a bang on your door in the middle of the night and your heart rate goes up, you will guide your body system into assuming you are scared. This way, your physiological reaction comes before your emotion. However, the theory is unable to account for several challenges and therefore critics like Walter Cannon one of the several critics questioned why physiological reactions were confined to specific emotions.

A study done by Marañón in 1924 found that physiological arousal is not enough to cause emotion. Only around two-thirds of participants who were injected with adrenaline reported physical symptoms. In addition, there were studies that indicate that not all emotions, save for the strongest and most basic ones, have been found to occur with specific physiological changes.

The theory was, however, also supported, in 1953, after AX noticed different psychological changes are related to different emotions. He basically meant that fear seems to be associated with the physiological effects of adrenaline, while anger appears to be associated with the effects of noradrenaline. Another study was done in 1981 also found distinct physiological reactions for anger, fear, happiness, and sadness. Advances in technology allowed psychologists to study bodily reactions, shedding more light on the James-Lange theory of emotion and addressing some of the compelling criticisms presented by Cannon. Using modern tools, researchers were able to demonstrate that some emotions involve different patterns of autonomic nervous system arousal and other bodily reactions.

Emotional Appraisal Theory

The appraisal theory states that emotions are extracted out from evaluations of events that, in turn, cause specific reactions in different people. An individual appraisal situation causes an emotional or affective response based on this specific appraisal.

Emotion appraisal theories have emerged from multiple sources, and they have all taken different Courses. What this means is that there is no singular appraisal theory that has emerged definitively within the emotion. In any case, they all compete to explain the emotional appraisal and its role in human emotion.

Appraisal theories have a non-conscious cognitive attribution as well as motivational input and physiological information. Each of them insists on an emotional state in response to a stimulus. However, the combination of the two depends on which appraisal theory you are looking at

One of the theories by Richard Lazarus defines two aspects; The appraisal of the significance of the event, and that of the individual, and its ability to respond. An example of how this theory fully depends on the individual is that your perception of things and especially emotional appraisal often leads to the end result emotion.

The theory runs on two basic approaches; The structural approach and process model. Both provide an explanation for the appraisal of emotions and explain in different ways how emotions can develop. In the absence of physiological arousal, we decide how to feel about a situation after we have interpreted and explained the phenomena. Thus, the sequence of events is as follows: event, thinking, and simultaneous events of arousal and emotion. The main controversy surrounding these theories argues that emotions cannot happen without physiological arousal.

Facial-Feedback Theory

This one focuses on the facial movement that is said to inspire emotion. The theory emphasizes on how facial expressions influence our own emotional experiences. A study by Strack in 1998 showed how participants who were asked to move their facial muscles into a smile. The study was under the guise of a cover story that did not mention emotional responses, were significantly more likely to report higher levels of amusement in response to a cartoon than control groups. In a different study, the theory was tested by having participants inject botox into the muscles associated with frowning. The result showed that the subjects exhibited decreased activation of brain areas associated with emotional processing while attempting to frown. This shows that the facial muscle movement accounts for at least some of the typically elicited emotion. The theory is fixated at the fact that facial expressions can have a big say in our emotional lives for both our expressed emotion and emotion read on someone else's face.

Chapter 2: Types of Emotions – 5 Common Emotions Experienced by Humans

Jealousy

Jealousy is a combination of different emotional reactions against the success of another person. The responses include; anger, fear, and anxiety brought about not being the primary owner of the privilege. Research has it that both women and men tend to be jealous because of various reasons. For example, when a woman believes her rival is more beautiful than her, it is likely to spark some jealousy. However, it is normal for practically everyone to experience some level of resentment. When caring about someone or something important, you may become anxious with the thought of losing the person or that something to somebody else.

There is pathological jealousy, also known as morbid jealousy. It is different from healthy suspicion in that it has a high intensity. It is so strong and tends to last for long. It is characterized by various things, such as paranoia and insecurity. An individual can quickly recover from the standard type of jealousy once they realize it is sort of unfounded. However, people who experience pathological jealousy take time to recover. These are because they are more obsessed with fears, and they always look for something to prove what they are suspecting will finally come to pass. Morbid jealousy is very destructive and unhealthy, especially in relationships. It will hinder you from the success or affection that you are so anxious. Whenever you get prone to morbid jealousy, you may likely succumb to depression, anxiety, self-destruction behaviors, and even develop suicidal thoughts.

What is the Leading Cause of Jealousy?

There are four leading causes of jealousy. One is having a poor self-image. This is where you tend to believe you do not look beautiful or handsome and that you are ugly. Chances are you will always be experiencing jealousy towards other people that you happen to meet, and they look way better than you.

The root cause number two is the lack of self-confidence. When you doubt yourself too much about the levels of your skills or the ability you have, you will be jealous. If you are entirely sure of what you are capable of, then you will have no jealousy feelings in you.

The next cause that can make you jealous is fear. Whenever you are afraid of what will happen, you may end up being lonely. This is because you do not want rejection or lose whatever you already have.

Also, insecurity can be a significant cause of jealousy, especially in relationships. Uncertainty is also brought about by having a poor self-image as well as a lack of self-confidence.

Is Jealousy a Sign of Love or Insecurity?

Jealous is an instinct. When you get to be genuinely in love with someone, in a matter of time, you will realize how beautiful the person is. You will value him or her. However, you may recognize someone else got their attention and time; you end up getting jealous. The moment jealousy strikes you, there will be a lot of insecurities between you and the other person.

However, rather than feeling insecure, it is always good to look at the things that can cause it. Address the little things in the relationship that are likely to worry you and work on what you can change within yourself. It is essential to know that you do not have the power to change somebody else. The other person can never be your moral responsibility. Instead, use the gut instinct of feeling jealous to be the right person and be able to strengthen the relationship with your mate.

Most people who experience jealousy have either been hurt in the past, or the present relationship is also not stable. When the other person lies or cheats, they have affected your trust. In most instances, when trust is broken, you become so jealous and insecure in your relationship. Love is always a two-way thing. No person should fight to keep the one person they love. If you find out that you do not trust them, then you are not in love.

Is Jealousy Mental Illness?

Morbid jealousy, or rather what we call pathological jealousy or in another term, delusional jealousy, is a mental disorder. The person affected is usually occupied with the thoughts that their partner in the relationship is cheating. However, there is no proof to back up the allegations — the person with the disorder experiences obsessions and some harmful delusions.

One suffering from the disorder may be violent, sabotage, stalk, or even cyberbully their partners. When one has the disorder, there are high chances of succumbing to drug abuse. Also, they may be affected by sexual dysfunction and too severe neurological illness.

How do you Fix Jealousy?

To be jealous is not a bad thing. It is the nature of human beings to feel resentful at any time. However, it becomes an issue when you get jealous and then wallow in it. It creeps in your life and affects your life too much. You will always be finding yourself very angry and bitter. Most people feel romantic jealousy others do feel jealous because of other people's strengths, successes, and healthful lifestyles. Below are some of the tips that can help you deal with jealousy.

Tips for Dealing with Jealousy

The first thing you should do is try and recognize the type of jealousy you have. When you are aware of it, you will be open to learning from it. One can make use of the feelings as an inspiration to grow well. Rather than getting buried in the jealousy, it is essential to do your best and do what it takes to be positive.

Also, let everything go. When one is convinced, you do not need the negative emotions in your life. Sit down somewhere, breathe in, and imagine the flow, then let it go like the wind. Also, try your level best always to manage your emotions healthily. Always be calm in every situation, even when they are negative.

It is an added advantage when you always try to remind yourself of the positive traits that you got. Have in mind that each and everyone got strengths and some weaknesses. Ensure the moment you start feeling jealous; you get to work on it before it gets so intense.

What is Depression?

Being depressed involves your body, moods, and thoughts you will be having from time to time. When one is affected by depression, the way they deal with life becomes different. The way you eat, how you feel, and interact with people becomes different. Depression is a disorder, and it is tough to deal with it all by yourself.

If you notice you have depression or someone is affected by it, advise them to seek medical help. When you get the right support, everything will be fine. Being depressed means, you will experience feelings of sadness that will last for an extended period. You will eventually lose interest in things that shape your life. Remember that people who are depressed do not acknowledge who they are. When one is depressed, it does not mean you have a weakness, or you are experiencing inadequacy. It is an illness that requires professional medical help.

There are three forms of depression. One is melancholia, which means significant distress. It can last for long if one does not seek good medical help. People suffering from melancholy do experience emotional and physical issues.

This is a bipolar disorder that can be a cause of massive mood swings. One is likely to feel overexcited at one time, and the next moment, they feel deficient. When it becomes severe, you may experience paranoia and hear voices that are not there.

The last one is dysthymia, which is an on-going depression, and in most circumstances, it begins when one is a child and lasts for years if not treated.

What Causes Depression?
There are quite several factors that can cause depression. One of the leading causes is genetics. When in your family, there is a history of depression, most likely, at one point in your life, you may experience it. Depression is thought to have complex traits. Therefore, it means that many genes that are different are bound to exert some effect.

Another one is drug and substance abuse. Most people, especially young adults who engage in drug abuse, are at a higher chance of getting major depression. Drugs may make you feel better temporarily, but in the ultimate results, they may make you get depressed. Certain medications can also lead to depression — especially some anti-retroviral drugs, steroids, and others that are used to treat acne. Also, having a significant illness such as cancer can affect a person on how they will cope with life.
Stress and conflicts can always make you feel tired and much drained physically. When you have personal conflicts or else disputes with your friends and family, one can suffer depression. Death of a loved one can also increase the chances of being depressed, especially if they were very close to you.

If one has ever experienced some sexual, physical, and emotional abuse there before, chances are they may be vulnerable to getting depressed at some point in life.

Finally, some events taking place in life phases and also personal problems can be significant causes of depression. They include; divorcing, losing jobs, no enough income, retiring, being lonely, among others. In additional environmental factors around, you can lead to depression. However, the bottom line is whatever the cause is. One needs to seek professional medical help before it is too late since it can negatively affect your personal life and derail you. It can be treated with the right guidance and medication.

What Are the Statistics of Depression?

Depression affects quite several people; the first group is the elderly. In 2009, the center for disease and control reported that seven million adults who are beyond sixty-five years do have depression. The survey was done in collaboration with the caregivers, and they said that most of the seniors have identifiable symptoms of depression.

Depression usually is more prevalent in women than in men. Mainly because of postpartum moods that often lead to severe depression, which is incapacitating and psychotic. However, the women who experience post-Partum depression in most cases may have experienced episodes that are depressive in the past before childbirth, but they did not get diagnosed. When a woman receives a major depressive disorder and not treated on time, it can increase the risks of bone fractures and osteoporosis.

Depression is also a significant cause of two-thirds of suicide deaths reported worldwide, especially for young people. From the year 2001 to 2017, the suicide rates have increased by over 30 percent.

In conclusion, people who experience other major illnesses do have a risk of developing depression. For example, twenty-five percent of patients with cancer do have depression. For patients living with HIV, depression is the second leading mental health condition. One in every three people who experience a heart attack, develop depression.

How to Treat Depression

The good news is that depression is treatable, and when diagnosed early, the patient will recover so fast. Once a patient visits doctors, they will be able to assess, and they will discuss the treatment option that is fit for you. There are two common ways to treat depression. They include cognitive behavioral therapy and antidepressant medication.

The antidepressant medication does change the electoral and chemical messages or signals sent to the brain. While the therapy helps to manage stress, improve social relationships, and help one to think positively. The medications help the patient to improve their moods, enhance their energy levels, and reduce problems associated with anxiety. If a doctor prescribes the drugs and they do not work, you may go back, and they will give way better one.

Through cognitive therapy, a person suffering from depression will be able to improve their life. One will feel way better, sleep well, be energized, socialize well, and think positively. The exercise mainly focuses on pleasing activities that will make you feel better. One can improve on the line of thought and have good feelings all through. The drugs will only work if the patient takes as prescribed by the physician.

It is always recommendable to seek medical advice the moment you realize you are experiencing some symptoms of depression.

The disorder impairs one's lifestyle and, if left untreated, may advance to more critical levels where gaining the normal mental state would be impossible. According to a recent study released by WHO, at least 350 million individuals suffer or are hospitalized from depression globally. Generally, in a group of 100 individuals, 4 suffer from depression.

Therefore, approximately 4.6% of the total world population suffers from depression.

Anybody, no matter the age, can suffer from depression. Kids may suffer depression if alienated with their mothers at a tender age. When the toddler fails to get the motherly intimacy, he can develop depression and become moonless. Youth can also get depressed from lack of basic needs, lack of employment, or being burdened by homework or from premature breakups. Also, adults can suffer depression from marriage and relationship issues, job loss or unemployment, while seniors can get depressed by lacking proper care and worrying too much about their children's life. The examples mentioned above are just factors that alleviate depression, but what are the exact causes of depression?

Causes of Depression

There is no definite cause of depression, but there are various already-determined causes grouped as medical, physical, or social. Life events are some of the major causes of depression. The type of event determines whether the depression will be short term or long term. In most cases, life events such as a sudden stop from work trigger a severe depression, which mostly occurs if one had not been mentally prepared for the issue. Most long-term life difficulties, such as being jobless, loneliness, and being in abusive relationships, trigger depression.

There are various personal factors that cause depression. They include family history, drug, and alcohol usage, medical illness, and an individual's personality. In some instances, depression runs in the family for generations that increase the genetic risk of suffering from this disorder. The possible explanation of this is exposure to similar factors that make family members susceptible to this disorder. However, being a family member of coming from a lineage with depression history doesn't guarantee that the individual will fall victim to suffering depression. According to medical practitioners, continued usage of drugs such as alcohol increases the risk of suffering from depression. Drug use disorder can cause or trigger the development of this depressive disorder.

Individuals' personality determines how vulnerable an individual is suffering from depression. Individuals with anxiety and worries a lot over small and mere issues tend to be more prone to the disorder. According to medical practitioners, abrupt changes in the neural circuit, located in the brain, can cause major depression. However, change in body chemicals is yet to be determined and its influence on depression if yet to be identified. Individuals experiencing body pains or suffering from painful long-term illness are more prone to depression.

Types of Depression
There are various types of depression categorized by the degree of effect or its duration from the development stage to being completely healed. Luckily enough, most depression symptoms are treatable through counseling and anti-depressive medications. The bipolar disorder is characterized by either high or low uncontrollable mood swings (Blatt 64). It is hard to differentiate between bipolar disorder and depression as most individuals seek treatment when having low moods but not when they have high moods. The premenstrual dysphoric disorder is another type of depression that mostly affects women a few days before and after their menstruation period and is mostly caused by hormonal imbalance. Cyclothymic disorder is another type of depression characterized by slightly higher and lower mood swings with mild symptoms than the bipolar disorder. The persistent depressive disorder is milder and long-term with a high potential of dismantling one's normal lifestyle.

What is Anger?
The chapter about anger has turned out to be the main topic of discussion for very many years now. Renown investigators like Berkowitz, who spend most of their time dealing with psychology, defines anger as a strong feeling of annoyance, displeasure, or hostility. It is also considered as a normal, healthy feeling that allows one to convey a message of reaction to a given situation. As much as it is reasonable to feel angry, the same attitude can be harmful if

you express it in a way that upset you or the people around you. Everyone has had a feeling of anger, and everybody has a way of dealing with the sentiment.

The bible has covered the topic of anger comprehensively. The verses that talk about anger are numerous, but we will only mention a few. In the book of proverbs, 15:1 states, "A gentleman answer turns away wrath, but a harsh word stirs up anger." The verse tells us that we should avoid responding to people with a negative attitude since it stimulates anger. Another famous verse about anger is proverbs 22:24 that strongly condemn us not to befriend hot-tempered people.

You might argue that anger is healthy, and you should express it maybe to earn respect, but the truth is that it can affect you negatively. According to Greil Brenner, anger causes separation. Anger scares people away from you. You are most likely to have a poor relationship with so many people, if not all around you. Studies have also shown that anger has a health effect on your health. Frequently operating at high levels of violence makes you vulnerable to diseases such as high blood pressure, diabetes, and can weaken your immune system.

What Are the Three Types of Anger?
Anger is a lot more complex topic since it has several classifications. According to Professor Ephrem Fernandez's research, anger can be categorized in bipolar dimensional expression. These include the mode of the anger, the direction of the anger, the anger reaction, the objective of anger, and anger impulsivity. There is a range of anger types, but the focus will be on the main three types. The most common one is the annoyance anger type. This one arises from so many day-to-day frustrations. This is the type of anger that happens to everyone. An excellent example of this type of anger is when a car veer next to you splashing water on you, or when you get yourself in a sensitive argument with your partner. It can also

happen when your kids are not listening and are stubborn. The list is long. It is easy to experience the annoyance anger type when you easily personalize other people's words daily. Surprisingly, upsets brought about by being triggered causes other people's problem to become part of your problem. A piece of good advice to help moderate this type of anger is that you should not take anything personally.

The second type of anger that you can quickly identify is aggressive anger. People at a higher level in a given group usually express this type of anger. The main goal of aggressive anger is to demonstrate express dominance, manipulation, intimidation, or control over others. While this type of anger might be useful when it comes to achieving a specific objective, expressing aggressive anger repeatedly is harmful. Regular expression of aggressive anger turns out to be a form of bullying, emotional abuse, and oppression. Most people consider aggressive anger as powerful but frequently make an individual insecure.

Another type of anger that you need to understand is justifiable anger. It is defined as having a moral outrage for seeing the injustice of the world. It can be environmental pollution, abusive behaviors at home, cruelty towards animals, or oppression of human rights. The good about justifiable anger is that it can be advantageous in the short run since it focuses on bringing change. As much as justifiable anger is beneficial, it can be harmful in the end as it hurts oneself when change is not affected. The only remedy of controlling this type of anger is by not waiting for change to take place. You either adapt to the ongoing situation or take the initiative of transforming the condition by yourself.

Is Anger an Emotion?
Most of the psychology studies consider anger as a natural and mature emotion expressed by all humans and that it is essential for survival.

Anger is an emotion that can be identified, but sometimes it can be hidden. For that reason, you must know some signs and symptoms of anger. One of them is being physically violent. You might find yourself pushing people away from you and even being aggressive. Another common symptom is feeling impatient, irritated, and hostile. When you are having a miserable social life and problem with your relationship, it is a good symptom of anger. Staying away from a specific situation is a good symptom of anger. Anger can be very harmful to oneself or the people around you. Therefore, you must manage the emotion before it escalates to an unmanageable level.

The best way to manage anger is by taking a deep breath and picturing relaxing images in your brain. This form of technology is called a relaxing technique. Visualizing relaxing experience and exercise like yoga helps you to calm your anger. Another way to manage your anger is by changing the way you think. Usually, an angry person has rational reasoning rather than irrational. It is advised that when you feel angry about something, try to communicate with your close friends about the issue. It is unwise to jump into conclusion before thinking through the situation. Having a healthy communication with your colleagues can help you cool down. You can also choose to visit a health professional, such as a psychologist who can help you come up with the right intervention to help you control your anger.

What is Fear

Fear is a natural feeling that everyone experiences frequently. It is something that you cannot avoid because it is a way of responding to severe sensations. It is easy to confuse fear with worry, anxiety, doubt, panic, and apprehension. The feeling of being afraid is the worst feeling that anybody would want to feel. It is uncomfortable, unpleasant, distressing, and at that point, you consistently try to come out of that situation. Everyone experiences fear in different ways; everyone is afraid of different things. This makes it challenging to come up with the right definition of fear.

Nevertheless, according to Arther J, Westermayr, fear is related to cowardice and that nobody wants to associate with scorn. He also defines fear as a collection of sensations and perceptions that signals you that something is threatening. The most confusing part about fear is that what you might find is threatening might not be frightening to your friend. For that reason, to fully understand fear, your definition needs to be centered around physical and internal emotions such as trembling, increased heartbeat, sweaty palms, shortness of breath, a feeling of despair and hopeless.

Why Do We Fear?
Some people would confidently tell you that fear is terrible; it is a sign of weakness, and that it is wrong. However, the truth is that fear is essential for our survival. The purpose of fear is to avoid dangers and challenging situations like diseases. It is vital since it allows you to live long and safely.

Surprisingly, there are fearful things that are common to every individual. Mostly, they are related to the environment, animals, fear of injection, and blood. Arachnophobia is a common fear majorly affecting women. Studies have shown that 1 out of 3 women are afraid of spiders. One out of five men is fearful of the sight of a spider. Some people panic by imagining or simply picturing the image of a spider. The question is, why is the number of people who are afraid of spiders so big? As far as there are so many different spider species, only a few of them pose a danger to humans. Thus, the best way to avoid this phobia is by learning and understanding more about spiders.

Another common form of fear is Ophidiophia. This is the fear of snakes. It is influenced by personal experience and culture. People believe that since some snakes are poisonous, all of them are harmful. Snakes in nature also provoke a disgust response, which generates fear to humans when spotted. Acrophobia is the fear of heights. Recent studies have shown that the fear of high areas affects a good percentage of the population. This fear is healthy because falling from top places poses a danger. People with this fear may try to go to high places frequently to get more comfortable with heights.

Therefore, we say without a doubt that the primary purpose of fear is to increase our chances of survival. For fear is what keeps us from danger and anything that could reduce our life span. Thanks to worry, we can increase our chances of survival. The difference between good and evil, what we eat and what we are not supposed to eat, how to protect ourselves from weather changes, and reducing the chances of contracting diseases are some of the many functions of fear. Putting almost all the challenges of not being afraid into consideration, then we have a small chance of survival in today's society. From infectious diseases to radioactive material, genetically modified foods to electronics and electrical pieces of equipment and industries, all modes of transport, and the dangers posed by both men themselves and animals at large. In that case, fear is reasonable and ever will be. Never be afraid of being afraid. It costs you nothing to be scared.

What is Fear in Psychology?

As discussed earlier, fear is what has enabled the survival of all living organisms. Therefore, for the next generation to survive, then fear should be placed on the top of the survival tactics list. As a result, there are two significant categories of fear. The first one is the emotional fear, which narrows down to the individuals, while the second one is biochemical fear that is universal.

In psychology, biochemical fear is characterized by sweaty hands and sweating, increased heart rates, and high adrenaline levels, among others. These reactions occur biochemically in the presence of danger. your body produces an automatic response of either fight or flight. They may have evolved through the evolution process. In animals, the biochemical reaction to fear is more or less the same. The aim is to either fight or flight. Thus, in psychology, the response is crucial for survival and the continuity of the lineage of individual and individual species as a whole.

The emotional fear experienced by an individual is also common and normal. Psychology has shown that emotional fear is high at a personal level. The brain is the most powerful organ in almost all living animals has fear characterized in more than one form. Since the brain controls what to be done, the fear may be positive being characterized by happiness and or excitement depending on the circumstance. For instance, when watching a scary movie or sky diving. Remember that the difference in feeling at this point relies on the mind of the individual.

Again, depending on the individual, fear may be harmful. The psychological reaction in an individual makes all the difference. Some people may like dangerous games and sports such as racing. The high speeds on the automobile may be termed unhealthy for one while others may have it as fun. The negativity relies on the brain and individual at large. Past experience also has a role to play at this point in life. Most people who have ever survived a road accident happen to be afraid of driving. However, due to unavoidable circumstances, they are forced to continue operating. This is how one's brain is powerful and is able to adapt to different situations and circumstances.

In psychology, there is no limit to the cause of fear. The experiences in fear vary from individual to individual, and so is the purpose of fear. The scientist has it that fear is an incredibly complex reaction, and they have not come to an agreement whether it is basically in the brain or the reactions to the surrounding of an individual that actually forces the brain to react the way it does. For instance, when you see a harmless snake, and you know that the snake is harmless, then how will your body and brain react to the situation. Then what will happen when the same snake is presented to you, and you do not know that the snake in question is either harmless or not? For that, the main cause of fear remains unknown and debatable.

In psychology, acclimation is when one is constantly exposed to the same threat repeatedly. The result is that the fear response in the individual in question happens to reduce. The biochemical and emotional fear response also tend to be within the normal range if not reduced. Others may use acclimation as a form of treatment. By others, once the fear has been overcome, they tend to seek even more thrilling activities that might put them in more fear.

Psychology of phobia has it that one tends to fear the fear response. This happens even when one is aware that the activity is may be harmless and may pose a minimal threat. The fear tends to worsen as the person in question stays in contact with the activity in question. Phobia is the worst kind of fear, and it is advised to be aware of his or her phobias. By being aware of them, you will be able to avoid them and avoid any further danger. Other than that, you may decide to work on your feet and, if possible, overcome it. The shortest way is through acclimation. This kind of fear response is most common in those who suffer from an anxiety disorder.

Treating phobia may sound more straightforward than it sounds. The most common way of treating phobia is through techniques such as systematic desensitization and flooding, as termed by experts. Experts have it that both methods work with the psychological of the body and the mental reaction. To begin with, systematic desensitization happens when one is systematically exposed to a series of his or her phobias. A good example is when say one has a fear of snakes, and then the best possible course of action is to begin by talking about snakes, the being exposed to pictures of the snakes, then finally having to handle a live snake. The reactions of the said person will determine whether he or she will move to the next class.

In flooding, the individual in question is exposed to his or her phobia but in a controlled environment and under supervision. The individual has to work his or her way up the ladder until the fear diminishes. This method has a higher success rate of succeeding, and it is highly recommended. As compared to systematic desensitization, the fear may express itself depending on the situation and environment and above all, depending on the time. Time is very crucial, and as much as the wise said that it heals old wounds, the same old wounds may be arisen based on the time. As a result, flooding is highly recommended. The techniques mentioned above are, therefore, to be carried out under the supervision of a trained and or a responsible individual. This is because they are very traumatic and hence requires the experience of a professional to be carried out.

What are the 10 Most Common Fears?

1. ***Arachnophobia is the fear of spiders and other arachnids.*** The main cause of this kind of fear dates back to our ancestors and evolution as a whole. This is because it is believed that the animal posed a threat to the earlier humans, and as adaptation stated, the man was adapted to fearing the animal in question to survive. The adjustment was then passed generation after generation to date.
2. ***Ophidiophobia is the fear of snakes.*** This is most commonly due to cultural beliefs and customs, personal experience, and at times evolutionary.
3. ***Acrophobia is the fear of heights.*** The result of this fear is the possibility of an attack and avoidance of high places.

The origin of this fear is yet to be determined besides the theory that suggests that traumatic experience and or environmental evolution where one tends to avoid areas that have a possibility of great danger in the event of a fall.

4. ***Aerophobia is the fear of flying.*** Despite the minimal possibility of a plane crash, the phobia is still evidenced in some people. Some of the characteristics of such phobia may include rapid heartbeat, sweating, trembling, and feeling disoriented. The most common treatment method for this kind of phobia is exposure. The individual is slowly and progressively introduced to flying.

5. ***Cynophobia is the fear of dogs.*** The phobia is mostly caused by personal experiences, such as being bitten by a dog in one's childhood. The possibility of such kind of fear may be carried to one's adulthood due to the trauma experienced. This kind of phobia may limit a person, such as avoiding walking on a particular street due to the presence of a dog. Daily activities will, at large, be affected.

6. ***Astraphobia is the fear of thunder, and lightning is experienced in some people.*** Some of the common characteristics of this kind of fear are rapid heart rate, shaking, and increased respiration.

7. ***Trypanophobia is the fear of injections.*** This kind of fear usually forces the affected people to avoid injections and doctors at large and at all costs. Like any other phobia, this kind of phobia is usually characterized by increased heart rate, extreme deeds, and at times, one might even faint.

8. ***Social phobia, also known as social anxiety phobia, is one that involves the fear of social situations.*** These kinds of people fear being watched and or being humiliated in front of others. Such fear, in most cases, usually develops during puberty and, if not taken care of,

may develop all through to adult life. The most commonly evident is the fear of public speaking.

9. ***Agoraphobia is the fear of being alone in a place where escaping seems impossible.*** Some of the causes are the situation, which might trigger a panic attack such as crowded places. It usually develops during one's 30s and beyond. It is most common in women.

10.

Mysophobia is the fear of germ and dirt. It might lead to excessive cleaning of places that tend to have bacteria and washing of hands compulsively. This kind of person might go to the extent of avoiding contact with other people.

Removing Fear from Mind

The only way to overcome your fear is to face them. This begins by knowing yourself. It includes your abilities and what you are good at, and most importantly, a backup plan in the event thing does not go as planned. A friend may play the role of a backup plan as he or she might come in handy. Exercise daily, as this will boost your confidence. Having faith and talking to others will also help. Further, medical therapy is also open, and one is advised to visit.

Stress and Worry

Stress is a natural human response when faced with challenging situations. Same as fear, the fight or flight action is triggered by the mind when stress is experienced. Stress might be positive or negative. It is positive when one's objectives are to be met; hence, more adrenaline is produced. For negative stress, depression is always experienced, and one might go to the extent of killing himself or herself.

What is Worry?

Worry is defined as a feel anxious about a potential problem.

Is Worry Same as Stress?
There is a difference since stress comes from the pressure of life, and worrying is thought-based, and it occurs inside the mind of a person.

What are 5 Emotional Signs of Stress?

1. ***Depression is one of the emotional signs of stress.*** A prolonged low mood mostly characterizes it. Some of the treatments of depression may include reaching out to professional therapists, going to support groups, and visiting a doctor.
2. ***Anxiety is another emotional stress sign.*** Overwhelming dread rather than a feeling of sadness mostly characterizes it. Some of the solutions to anxiety may include visiting a doctor, reaching out to a mental professional, and natural approaches are present for consideration.
3. ***Irritability is also another emotional sign of stress.*** These are common traits in people who are stressed. A variety of strategies can help manage anger, and having anger management classes will also help.
4. ***Memory and concentration problems also play a part as a sign of stress.*** It is characterized when an individual is having trouble remembering things, and this is most common when the person I question is stressed. Various lifestyle changes and improving diet may help.
5. ***Mood swings are also a common sign of stress.*** Some of the solutions may include celebrating with friends, enjoying nature, and reducing stress as a whole.

What are the Symptoms of Anxiety and Stress?

1. ***Excessive worrying is one of the many symptoms of anxiety and stress.*** This kind of worry is always severe making it impossible for one to concentrate.
2. ***Feeling agitated is also a symptom of anxiety and stress.*** This usually happens because your brain believes that you are in danger.
3. ***Restlessness is also a characteristic symptom of anxiety and stress.*** These usually happen in most children and teens. These are some of the key symptoms that doctors usually look for.
4. ***Fatigue also plays a role as a symptom of anxiety and stress.*** Other than the usual causes of fatigue, keeping an eye on the cause will clear every doubt on whether it is as a result of causes or a symptom.

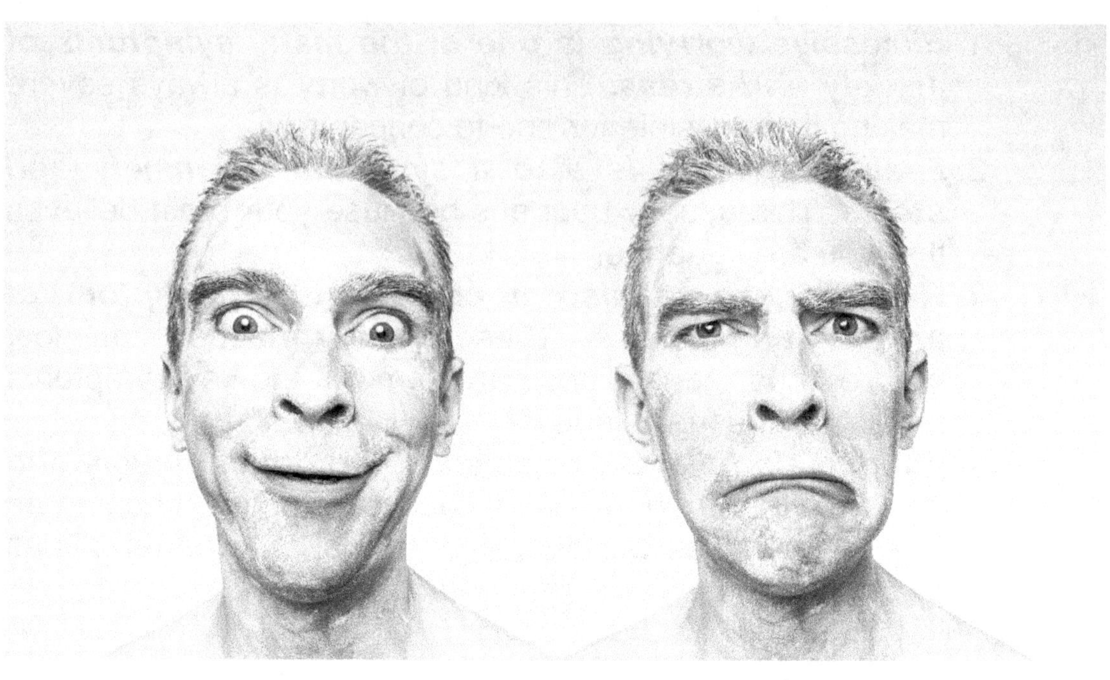

Chapter 3: How to Condition Your Emotions

Have you ever positively or negatively responded to the changes in the environment? Maybe associating food and the plate, or even the smell of gasoline with the pleasant tour you had the other day or in your childhood. All of these are examples of conditioned emotions. Therefore, emotion condition is the learned emotional reaction towards a conditioned stimulus.

When you feel anxious or loved, happy for something sad, or even affectionate towards various circumstances, you are experiencing conditioned emotion. You might have noticed that this response is associated biologically with the reaction of the organism.

The autonomic nervous system is responsible for controlling all the emotional responses. In an average person, the sympathetic nervous system plays a role in various conditioned emotions. The emotions include anxiety, panic attack, and stage flight. In response to these, the system will activate either fear or fight. The body will biologically increase your heartbeat, weakness in the knees, and even sweating. Have you ever experienced these conditions? Then it is a result of emotional conditioning.

Why Do You Need Emotion Conditioning?

Imagine burning because you did not respond to the sight of fire. It is dangerous. Or a boy is mauled by a hungry animal since he could not hurriedly react to the sight of a cheetah. Therefore, emotional conditioning is vital for your survival.

First, conditioned emotion will motivate you to take action. If you see a lion, a conditioned stimulus associated with killing people, you will run and hide away from it not to be killed. In another instance, if the exam is approaching, and you know that you have not prepared for it in the right way, conditioned emotion will prompt you to take the action of studying extra hard to avoid falling.

Second, it helps you make decisions. According to research, people with the inability to experience emotions have the problem of making sound decisions. Have you ever voted? What made you vote for the leader? You will discover that most of the choices you make rely on your conditioned emotions. Look at the beautiful dress you like, what do you associate it with? The party you went to or your dad gave it to you as a birthday present. You take hot coffee on a chilly morning and cold soda during a hot summer day to reduce the heat and thirst from your body because you already know how to handle such a day.

You understand other people because of conditioned emotions. When you come across a shivering boy, you will notice that he needs warm conditions. If you find a hissing animal, you know that it is angry and defensive; therefore, back off and avert the danger.
The same way you understand others because of conditioned emotions, they too understand you through the same feelings.

Does Conditioning Affect Emotion?

Conditioning is the main reason for the change in emotions. Due to conditioning, therefore, the body responds to the various stimuli in different ways, mainly positively and fears. The fear results in different phobias. When you associate a steep hill with falling, you will, therefore, fear steep places even when you will not fall. You fear the dog since you associate it with biting, or it bit you sometime back. You, therefore, will back off from it even when it will not bite you. Conditioning significantly affects emotion.

Can Human Emotions be Conditioned?

From the study contact on an infant, Albert, a scientist, says that it is clear that you can condition human emotions. In his example, when a rat was associated with a loud bang, the boy withdrew from it and even started to cry.

From the findings, therefore, you can condition human emotion. From common knowledge, a lion is known to prey on other animals. Thus, when people see it, they cry and run away. You will always run away from a place associated with danger. When you see a vehicle off the road to the ditch, you shout, moan and groan even if nobody is already hurt.

What is an Emotional Response?

When you react from an outside stimulus, you will have emotionally responded to it. An emotional response is the reaction of your body towards a situation given from an external source.
This emotional response is one of the many emotions people experience and has two main procedures, Stress reaction, and grief.

What Area of the Brain is Involved in Conditioned Emotional Responses?

Emotion Conditioning by Using Music

Music has a significant effect on human emotion. You may not even notice how the music has changed the feeling, but it affects the human brain and hence, the emotions. The main parts of the brain affected by music are the hippocampus, amygdala, and the dopaminergic pathway. You see, you might be dancing enjoying the music, sometimes you cry mourning from a sorrowful song. Remember how a given pop or love song reminds you of the nostalgic days you had.

Why Does Music Have an Emotional Effect?

As noted earlier, music has the power to evoke strong emotions within people. You will notice that the effect has been perceived to the extent that it is difficult to see the change if you are not very careful. This field of music and its relation to emotion is still vast for one to study. Music evokes feelings of nostalgia, sadness, happiness, and love, among others. Is it true that it affects you? Which emotions does it evoke in you?

Why Does Music Move Us?

You will notice that music touches all the parts of your life. It evokes several emotions to the extent that you tend to react based on the feeling you evoke. Sometimes you cry and weep, remembering how the situation was adverse in the road accident or the fire outbreak, yet a piece of given music was playing. Every time you hear that particular song, you have to recall it.
Music has played several roles in your emotions.

Which Emotions Does Music Evoke?

Music evokes emotions in your life. Have you ever felt to cry after listening to a particular song? Or does another one makes you fall in love again? Can you recall the song that reminds you of the happy or bad times you ever had?

How Does Music Help Express Feelings?

Though many people believe that words cannot express emotions, musical words have powers to move mountains in the heart. Many time s when a musical code is touched. It reveals a feeling from the singers. Some artist you will agree with this, compose the song depending on the situations they are passing through. Some sing and even cry on the stage; others even leave the arena due to excess emotions. It is true that in many circumstances songs, especially the dirge and love songs express feelings.

How Music Affects Your Brain?

Music has an impact on the brain in various areas. The first one is the amygdala that is responsible for the emotions in humans. Second is the hippocampus that is an elongated ridge on the floor of lateral ventricles of the brain. This part of the brain is thought to be the center of memory, autonomic nervous system, and the emotions in your mind.

You don't listen to music to get the emotions but many times music is the one that evokes emotions

Thoughts

Music has affected the mind of humanity for centuries now based on the study. The memory of many people associates a particular piece of music with a given experience. What is your experience, can you recall the feeling for that piece? Music evokes various thoughts in your mind. Sometimes on the religious songs, some people might think of the existence of the spirits. Are you in agreement that music affects your thoughts? You should note that.

How Can You Condition Your Emotions by Thoughts?

You cannot control what you think, but you can determine what to do or not. From this statement, you might indeed think of running away because of fear, but the thought and mind should always guide you on what to do in any particular circumstances. It is still essential to react based on the thought and not merely because you don't feel like doing so.You don't need to feel right for you to respond to a particular stimulus. You might feel thirsty, yes, but is it the right time to take water? The thoughts and mind should always dictate when to take any action. Always put your mind and thoughts before emotions for better survival.

Conditioning the Mind

The mind has forever played a vital role in our lives since humanity came into being. That is why humanity is different from other animals. A positive mindset will always dictate the emotions you experience. The mind is responsible for the attitude. When the mind decides that you will not fear anything, you will not worry, thus controlling the emotions. If you choose not to love anybody at a particular time, you would therefore not like it. If you decide that you won't cry in any situation, take the police officers as examples, the emotion will always incline.

Classical Conditioning

This kind of conditioning is the process of learning through association. In this condition, you have to link stimuli so that you can arrive at a learned response either in an animal or a human. According to the study that was carried out by John Watson, classical conditioning cuts across all human reactions. In this type of conditioning, there is no existence of consciousness or even the mind. When a rat is associated with noise for several times, you will always respond to sound at the sight of the rat. This happens unconditionally.

According to the argument, if you take several fresh human brains randomly to different places under different situations, you will raise the human beings of your liking despite the presence of talents. If you need a doctor form any child, give it the necessary conditions, and it will become a doctor.

How Does It Help in Conditioning Your Emotions?

Classical conditioning helps in conditioning of the emotions. For example, if you train the child never to fear a dog, provide the necessary conditions, and the child will even sleep with the dog on the same animal under the same blanket. The same applies to monkeys and any other thing that stimuli fear in a human. The opposite is exact that if you train a child to live knowing that a particular condition is adverse, they will, therefore, live to fear it.

Work Environment

What is Positive Reinforcement at Work, and how does it affect your emotions?

You show Positive reinforcement when good work or behavior is rewarded. Reward your employees when they do good work. According to the study, when you reward good practice, it will tend to reoccur. In the working environment, therefore, it is always important to acknowledge and reward good behaviors and efforts to maintain such behavior.

When you reward your employees, they will feel motivated and happy. You will find out that the emotions of the workers towards your work will be positive, happy, and ever anxious to work hard to maintain the excellent work. Remember that the size of the prize does not matter, but what matters is when you give your employers the rewards in the right environment and the right way.

Its Effectiveness Compared to Negative Reinforcement

Positive reinforcement is when you add a stimulus so that you can increase positive behavior. On the other hand, negative reinforcement is reducing the adverse stimulus to encourage positive reinforcement. An example of positive reinforcement is when you give a bonus to a hardworking employee. In negative reinforcement, you will make the overcrowded offices spacious and making them conducive for the workers.

All in all, all the reinforcements result in improved behavioral outcomes. In positive reinforcement, you find out that it is very natural as it involves desirable behaviors. On the other hand, negative reinforcement can look undesirable as it depends on the employee's conduct. In negative reinforcement requires you do remove what is existing because of the condition of your employees' behavior. In positive, it is essential to improve on the current behavior.

How to Give Positive Reinforcement to Employees

You can reward your employees in various forms. Reward them through voice growth and self-efficacy, empowerment, and approval. Never assume that the workers know that they are doing a great job, approve them of the work they do. Always give positive rewards for quality work. Provide motivational speakers for them; provide them with a chance to air their views. Also, encourage them to share the well-done job with their colleagues.

Reward them too through benefits, time off, monetary, advancement, and educational support. Always give them a competitive salary depending on performance. Always give them a monetary bonus, depending on the performance. Whenever they are sick, feel free to provide them with paid sick leave. Pay for quality health benefits. Give your employees discounts and even added vacations to motivate them the more. Encourage your performing employees to advance their education and reimburse them on the same.

Also consider them for work and life balance, health, family needs, emotional well-being. You need to create a conducive environment at your workplace for them. In this case, bring in motivational speakers to encourage them and motivate them to work even harder. Let the working hour be flexible. Encourage them to have time for socialization and family. If possible, let there be a daycare service at the firm for the children. You can include a gym and several social facilities at the firm. Increase for them the time to go for lunch and even relax from the pressure at work. Let the working environment be as conducive as possible.

Techniques and Strategies for Using Positive Reinforcement with Adults

When you use positive motivation, you will achieve very much in increasing motivation, satisfaction, and productivity in your firm. If you offer your employers with appraisals in various levels of work, they will develop morale for work and continue with the desired behavior. As a good employer, you should enhance employee motivation by supporting their value of work at an individual level. Below are some of the technics you can use in developing positive reinforcement in adults.

First, trust and respect them. Always deliver reinforcement with a lot of respect, and hence, the two will work mutually.

Second, it is essential to have realistic optimistic. Don't just be anxious without setting realistic goals. Always promote positive behavior but consider setting realistic goals. This basically depends on the employee acquired skills and the level of work.

Third, inspire and motivate your workforce. You can even call the motivational speakers to enhance them on the importance of maintaining positive behavior at work.
You should also give them a meaningful and sincere response. Always give genuine feedback as this will create trust from the employees. Do not ever offer positive feedback for the sake of doing so.

Another way is by giving regular responses. Always reward good work on time and at regular intervals. The employees should notice that and hence work towards achieving the rewards in time.

You can always promote an exceptionally performing employee by giving them leadership roles. Still, convey the underlying message that hard work fosters hope. Allow them always hope for the best when they work hard.

Also, model the desired behavior. Always walk the talk. Let your junior see what you want in you. They will quickly full suit without complaining.

Promote employee self- efficacy. Those willing to ascend the leadership ladder can quickly go up provided they meet the desired qualifications.

When rewarding your juniors, always use a meaningful reward system. The system should come up with significant incentives that are used to reward positive behavior. The reinforcement can be social, token, or even economic ones depending on the desires of the receivers.

Communicate clearly on what to expect after what. For the mechanism to work, it is essential to let both the managers and employees to know what to expect once they achieve the set goal.

You should also give your employees an intellectual challenge. Have you ever thought about it? Were you challenged at your workplace? You will notice that it is always essential to test the employee's intellect before rewarding for a positive response.
Give the meaning behind the message. As a good leader, you should always go beyond behavior reinforcement. The employees should comprehend the reason behind the rewards and reinforcements.

Have a listening ear for your employees. You won't be happy if someone doesn't want to listen to your views. In the same way, therefore, be a good leader who listens and cares about the grievances from your juniors.

Let the reinforcement is specific. The employer should know where they did well and where they need to improve. When it is such specific, they can know what to do in the future.

Let the mechanism promote teamwork. If you reinforce teamwork behavior, you will encourage the whole team to work in collaboration and hence, improved the work environment.

Major on responsibility. Give everyone a role to play. This will develop in them a sense of their performance and accountability.

8 Ideas for Implementing Positive Reinforcement

It is always vital to implement positive reinforcement at work. You will achieve them by doing the following:

- Make sure that your workplace is still clean. Dirty reduces positive behavior.
- Encourage innovation among the employees; let them also come up with their way of solving problems.
- Encourage the sharing of skills. Whenever one has acquired expertise either through seminars or workshops, encourage them to share them.
- Fill your office with life. These can be plants like the flowers, the fish making it highly rewarding.
- Consider lunch break as a great matter. You can even increase the time so that the workers can have enough time to rest after lunch.
- Always be informed about the current events. This helps in approaching matters from an informed point of view.
- Encourage your employees to take breaks as they relieve them from the pressure at work.
- Encourage employees with passion. Support them to achieve their goals, especially when they need some material and financial assistance.

<u>**Reward Ideas for Adults**</u>

It is essential to base the rewards on the individual employee's needs and interests. Some of the ways to achieve this are by:

- *Having a massage on the firm*
- *Fitness classes on the premise*
- *The lovers of beer should get it freely*
- *Recreation centers in the company*
- *Regular recognition among other services like free parking*

Chapter 4: Effects of Emotions in Your Daily Life – How Emotions Can Build or Break You

Emotions play a major role in concern about how we think and behave. They are mental states associated with the nervous system. They are brought about by chemical changes usually associated with thoughts, feelings, behavioral responses, and a degree of pleasure or displeasure. The emotions we feel in our daily lives influence the decisions that we make both for ourselves and our families. They have a great impact on our lives since they can build us or break us depending on how we perceive their feelings. Here are the main types of emotions and how they build our lives by building us or breaking.

Fear

Fear is a powerful emotion experienced by all humans. It alerts us about the presence of danger in our environments. It involves chemical reactions that affect our brains when we come up across certain situations. People have different types of fears regarding personalities. Other fears are caused by trauma, past experiences, or fears of something else like loss of control.

It is completely difficult to understand what is fear. However, the impacts of it are completely evident in our lives. Many people argue that fear is the greatest path to the darkest sides. It leads to anger, which directs us to hate and eventually to sufferings. Some of the greatest leaders of the world, like Barrack Obama, had to do away with their fears for them to be successful. They defied all the odds of fear, took all the courage, and at the end of it, all achieved their dreams and goals.

Fear ruins people. It has killed young ambitions, destroyed relationships, killed businesses destroyed faiths, destroyed negotiations, and killing lives. It becomes our obligation to understand our fears and come up with ways on how we can face them and reduce them. However, fear can also help us build our lives by helping us escape from coming dangers. Fear helps us to understand the chances of any dangers ahead, defend ourselves from them an advantage to ourselves.

Happiness

Being happy is not only a feeling of feeling good. Various researches have shown that happiness does not make us only feeling good but also makes us healthier, nicer to ourselves and other people, and be more productive in our daily activities. Therefore, everyone needs to feel happiness emotion to live a comfortable life.
Living a happy life is not hard. It does not entail denying negative emotions or trying to fake happiness by being joyful at all times. As humans, it's common for us to feel negative emotions of anger, frustrations, sadness, among other negative emotions. However, happiness helps us to cope with these bad times to experience the best possible life overall.

According to research from Warwick University, happy people are more productive as compared to their peers. From the research, happy people are 11% more productive. Happiness also helps us to avoid some of the lifestyle diseases like depressions, which is a leading killer disease in the current environment. However, excessive happiness emotion might negatively affect us. It may result in over-confidence, which makes us less attentive and creative in our daily activities. These negative aspects of happiness emotion destroy our lives by breaking us and making us feel demotivated.

Love

Love is the heart's emotion. It is a good emotion. It sometimes makes us do crazy things that help us to build our lives, but in other cases, it can cause us to do things we are not proud of and as a result, end up breaking our lives. Everyone wants to be loved or to be in love. It's an emotion of compassion and fullness that we receive from our lovely ones. Love for oneself is also a crucial factor. It leads to the acceptance of ourselves despite our inferiority.

Love emotion plays a major role in our lives, both positively and negatively. It has a major impact on our health systems. From previous researches, each time that you express your love to someone, the brain releases hormone serotonin, which plays a major role in improving our health systems. Love also creates closer ties with our friends and families, which creates stronger relationships, thereby building our lives greatly.

Love can also greatly break our lives. Currently, it is a major cause of suicides among the young generation from the feeling of not being loved and not accepting yourself. It contributes to depressions between individuals, which results in personal stress, psychological problems, and mental diseases. From the above points, love emotion should be not a bed of roses. Always be cautious with other people's hearts regarding the love that you offer since it greatly affects them positively or negatively by either building or breaking their lives.

Anger

Anger is a powerful emotion characterized by feelings of antagonism, hostility, frustration, and agitation towards other people. It plays a major role in in-flight management. The feelings of the emotion of anger are easily noticeable from an individual. For example, one can display the emotion by frowning, talking with a strong stance, yelling, physiological responses such as sweating and turning red or through aggressive behaviors such as throwing objects.

Most individuals perceive anger as a negative emotion which only ruins relationships and break down our lives. However, anger has positive elements in our lives. It is constructive since it helps us to clarify the issues not clear with us in a situation. It can also motivate us to find solutions to the problems that are a bother to us.

However, excessive anger is harmful to our daily lives, especially when expressed in ways that are harmful and dangerous towards the life of others. Numerous cases of deaths and permanent injuries are being recorded daily as a result of uncontrolled anger. The effects of anger emotion have also spread to coronary heart diseases and diabetes among other dangerous diseases. It's, therefore, our role as humans to come up with strategic methods of dealing with our anger to control the harmful effects of anger emotion.

Pride

When we think of deadly sins, pride is arguably one of them. However, pride is not as bad as people think. Sometimes pride helps us to build our lives and also improve the lives of others. It is natural for a person to feel the emotion.

The accomplishment of certain goals and objectives tends to make us feel proud of our own efforts. It is from the pride that we feel motivated and desire to achieve more goals, which help us to build our lives. On the other hand, emotion has led to the downfall of many individuals, families, and dynasties. Pride people are usually arrogant and do not follow instructions set aside. There is even a saying the pride comes before a fall.

Guilt

Guilt is an emotion that signals us when our actions or inactions have caused or might cause harm to another person. The feeling of guilt is unique from the emotion of sadness. It combines feelings of humiliation, anxiety, shame, and frustration. The emotion greatly affects us by affecting our sense of self-worth and self-esteem.

The feeling of guilt in an individual can adversely affect a person. It makes us avoid other people due to the fear that we wronged them, which is not necessary. Some people are triggered to punish themselves for sins that they did not commit. It lowers our self-esteem when we try to figure out how the other party perceives us which results in stress and eventually depression. It's therefore good for one to open up to the other party and ask for forgiveness rather than keeping the harmful emotion.

On the other hand, emotion helps us to shape our lives in several ways. It helps us to build our personalities towards life. If you have wronged someone, the feeling of guilt punishes you such that one will try to avoid committing a similar sin toward another person.it also helps you to achieve our goals. Our decisions do not please all individuals. We have to get stronger and learn how to face feelings of guilt. However, it's always right to do what is right and acceptable to you to avoid feeling guilty.

Sadness

Sadness is an emotion that all people experience from time to time. Its characterized by feelings of disappointment, grief, hopelessness, and dampened moods. It is expressed in different methods and the most common ones being crying, withdrawal from others, quietness, and low morale. It is normal for one to feel sad. However, excessive sadness destroys our lives since it leads to stress, which is the mother of many depressions. Sadness is also an important emotion that helps you build your life. When we are sad, we tend to move away from the factor contributing to the sadness, which might be an impending danger.

The emotions that we perceive have clear impacts on our daily activities. It hence becomes our role how to control them to ensure that they build our lives and destroy them. One should also be cautious with other people's emotions since, in a way, it might adversely affect them.

How Emotions Help You to Survive and Thrive

Emotions guide your lives in numerous ways. Most of you do not understand to which extent emotions drive your thoughts and behaviors. They impact your lives through a million ways, either positively or negatively. Emotional intelligence assists you in understanding, use and managing your emotions in positive ways hence helping you to relieve stress, communicate effectively, empathize with your other individuals, overcome challenges, and reduce chances of conflicts among individuals. According to recent researches, emotional intelligence is more important than intelligence quotient since it predicts over 54% of the variation in success, quality of life health, and relationships. They play a significant role in helping you survive and thrive, as shown by the paragraphs below.

Help Build Stronger Relationships

By understanding your emotions, how to manage them, and express them, you can build stronger relationships with your friends. This is because you are able to express your feelings positively to the other party. Emotions also help you to communicate effectively without fear both at work and in personal lives, which aids in building strong relationships with other people. One should try to figure out other individuals' emotions. This helps to avoid hurting them, which significantly destroys relationships. Without strong relationships, success becomes hard to achieve. World-leading business entrepreneurs and leaders associate their success to healthy relationships that emanate from understanding their clients' emotions. For you to survive and thrive in the modern world, it is therefore vital to understand the role of emotions.

They Affect Decision Making

Emotions are the root course of your daily decisions. They affect not only the nature of the decision but also the speed at which you make the decision. Take, for example, the emotion of anger. It leads to impatience in most people, which results in rash decision making. In other cases, if you are excited, one is more likely to make quick decisions, not considering their implications, which could be dangerous. When afraid, the choices that you make could be clouded by uncertainty and might be poor decisions.

The decisions that you make daily determine the success of your lives. Take for example, in a negotiation; if the decision you make is affected by the fear of emotion, the outcome will be poor. This is opposed to if, during the negotiation, there was happiness emotion. The results are positive, and the parties end up making lasting relations with benefits to both the parties. It's, therefore, essential to apply emotional intelligence before making any decisions for the success of your lives.

They Improve Your Health

There are many physical benefits associated with your emotional well-being. Take, for example, the emotion of falling in love leads to relaxation and contentment and also boosts the growth of new brain cells, which improve your memory capacity. Previous researches have shown that the expression of happiness emotions through laughter not only boosts your moods but also increases life expectancy. Positive emotions also help you to reduce the chances of contradicting emotion-related diseases like depression and high blood pressure, which are some of the leading sources of death. It's, therefore, becomes vital for people to take care of their emotions to increase their chances of survival and thriving in life.

They Motivate You to Take Actions

When faced by a situation, emotions help you to take steps. Take an example when you are about to sit for an exam, one might feel a lot of anxiety as tom whether they will pass the examination and also how it will affect the final grade. It's from the emotion that one is compelled to study hard to pass, which leads to success. Always consider taking positive actions towards emotions for you to live a comfortable and successful life.

Emotions Help You to Avoid Danger

According to naturalist Charles Darwin, emotions are believed to be adaptations that allow humans to survive and reproduce. They serve as an adaptive role by motivating you to act quickly and take quick actions to increase your chances of survival and success. A good example is when you experience fear as a result of a coming danger like a dangerous animal or a possible threat. You are more likely to free from the threat by running, which increases your chances of survival. When angry, you are more likely to confront the source of the irritation which increases the rate of your survival.

They Help You to Understand Other People

Life without friends could be very much dull and with many problems. You require help from one of your friends since no person can survive independently. Emotions help you to understand the people that you interact with on a daily basis, which plays a significant role in determining the chances of your success. By understanding other people, you learn about their weaknesses, and hence, when interacting and dealing with them, you avoid situations that would hurt them. By understanding other people, you can respond appropriately and build strong and mutual relationships with friends, families, and loved ones. This leads to your success and also helps you to thrive in hard situations.

Enhance Understanding

Your emotions act as a means of communication to the society. When you are interacting, it's always good to express your emotions to them to help them understand you better. For example, somebody's language and signals such as facial expression and body movements aid others in understanding you more. Take an example when sick you express your pain through emotions such as sadness, which informs your friends that you require the services of a doctor. This is an important aspect that increases your chances of survival and success. Without emotions, life would be much difficult to thrive and succeed.

They Build You as A Strong Leader

World great leaders and business entrepreneurs are known to have a common trait that is they understand other people's emotions. Understanding others' opinions not only helps an individual to influence others but also, it's a tool that helps to inspire them. It, therefore, becomes possible to build trust among your workers and also develop teamwork among them leading to the success of your organizations. As a leader, it's therefore fundamental for you to learn the emotions of your peers and workmates.

They Help You to Apologize When Wrong

Many people do not understand the importance of apologizing when faulty. When wrong your emotions of the guilt towards the affected party make you apologize. By apologizing, you can re-establish your dignity to those that you hurt; it helps you to repair the broken relationship with your friends and also helps to let other people know that you are not proud of your actions, but instead, you are sincerely sorry for your actions. It's from your emotions that you apologize. The apologies are a great catalyst to your success in life by the restoration of broken bondages and families.

They Help You to Cope with Difficult Life Situations

Your emotions help you to deal with hard life situations. When a situation like death strikes one of your loved ones, the emotion of sadness and anger falls on you. The emotions make you express your responses through methods such as pushing others away, crying or even blaming yourselves for hard situations. According to research, expressing your emotions through crying helps you to get relieved, and eventually, over time you can thrive back in life.

They Boost Your Creativity

Emotions are usually connected to your thoughts. When in a hard situation, your emotions trigger your brains to take rapid actions to counter the situation. Take an example when attacked by a dangerous animal; the emotion of fear triggers the brain to search for any weapon that would kill the animal. Also, when in an interview, the emotion of anxiety to get the job motivates you to think hard for you to acquire the posts. In many situations, creativity from your emotions leads to your success in the workplace and also at your homes with your families.

They Help You to Accept and Appreciate Yourselves

When you achieve your goals and objective in life, emotions of joy, happiness, pride tend to overwhelm you. The emotions help you to appreciate yourselves more from work well done. Recognizing yourselves motivates you to do more and more, which results in success in life. Without self-appreciation, it becomes difficult for other people to appreciate you or recommend you to other people who would have helped you much.

From the paragraphs above, it's evident that emotions play a crucial role in your success. They greatly influence how you interact with others and determine how you thrive at the workplaces and your homes. It, therefore, becomes much essential to control your emotions so as not to affect others negatively, which can result in your downfall.

Chapter 5: How to Manage Your Emotions

Many are times that you find yourself in situations likely to cause anger, hate, and resentment, which may be followed by a reaction likely to cost you. Managing emotions is the ability to control your feelings successfully. This powerful capability undergoes the process of changing your thoughts and feelings', ensuring any outburst is prevented.

Are Emotions Manageable?

Emotions are a mental state connected to the nervous system brought about by chemical changes often inspired by your behavioral responses, feelings, thoughts, and any degree, whether of pleasure or displeasure. Being emotional is not necessarily associated with sadness or loss, either way, they are manageable, but this will depend on the individual.

Imagine yourself in your work station, either a business or an office, halfway through the day, your senior or boss walks in and starts yelling at you complaining of your work ethics and professionalism. All these he is telling you is hearsay, and not a bit is valid. The temptation to yell back will cross your mind because all you are being accused of is not based on any true grounds, but for the sake of keeping your job, you will have to take yourself through a process known as stop, drop, and process.

Stop: The first step is often the hardest because it totally depends on your will power and your ability to untie yourself from the strong emotions and the urge to get back. Manageability at this point calls for stopping the thought process and thinking about the situation at that very point. By stopping, this buys you time, and the few minutes will let the anger and vengeance thoughts to fade away.

Drop: By dropping the intensity of your emotions, now you can engage in a sober talk if there is room for you to hold a conversation. If not, the other party at this point is likely not to continue yelling at you and blaming you for the false accusations.

Process: This is the third and last step of getting yourself out of the quagmire. Your boss has stopped blaming you at this point, and he now expects you to respond. Once you have evaluated the situation in your mind and looked at the repercussions of any answers you give, you are good to go ahead and tackle the huddle in front of you. By processing, your emotional intelligence has kicked in at this point, and even though you still hurt from the little encounter, your emotions are well managed and responded too intelligently and on a sober mind.

Emotions are manageable and controllable too. Your response will highly depend on the need to survive and the brain process advised by the steps; stop, drop, and process. Also, knowing your own feelings as well as those of others plays a big role in emotional manageability. The success of management is possible in many situations especially once you are aware of your feelings and values. If it is a situation where your emotions are brought about by joy, you are not likely to have an angry outburst. However, this too should be managed to avoid any negative repercussions or results.

Let's say you are at the airport and your sister Susan arrives just when reports at the airport say that there is a plane that has been involved in an accident and it is not recognizable, and the crew members kindly ask you and others at the waiting station to keep calm and wait for more reports. Once you see your sister Susan alight the plane, you start shouting and jumping as you call out her name, not minding other bystanders who have not seen any of their family members or heard from the airport. Emotions of joy are a positive thing, but you have to manage them by considering your surroundings and other people's feelings towards your reaction or response to a situation. Your underlying beliefs about emotions whether or not you are aware of them can affect your happiness in life.

What is Anger Management?

Usually, when an annoying situation faces you, hurts, or even humiliates you, you are prone to anger, and most likely you will react to the situation. Anger management is the use of skills that help in recognizing the signs and triggers of anger and assist in expressing yourself in a calm and collected manner and intentionally refusing to be controlled by anger. Usually, anger management is necessary where the emotion of anger is likely to cause problems. Anger can be both negative or positive depending on the circumstance.

Anger management will depend on the type of anger you are ailing from; Passive aggression; This is when there is no confrontation is involved, and you don't want to admit that you are angry this may be followed by silence, sulking, and even going about your business like everything is fine.

Open Aggression; In this situation, you are likely to lash out in rage and aggression. In this case, you may cause verbal or physical damage.

Assertive Anger; If your anger is assertive, you will be in a position to express yourself. Your anger here is expressed directly and not in a threatening or abusive way. You can solve the situation at hand and probably even find a way forward. These types of anger all require different skills in management.

Anger management is advised by the fact that the responsibility for your emotion is projected on the other party or parties. This is why it is essential for you not to cause further damage, whether verbal or physical. Now, through your mind and thought process, you can change the person or deed that makes you believe caused you anger.

Are There Any Anger Management Tests?

In case you decide to undergo an anger management program or even class, an anger management test is used to evaluate and help you understand your anger and at the same time determine areas that the client needs to improve on. This is usually in order to assist you to arrest uncontrollable emotions and feelings of anger to prevent the situation at hand from becoming worse. By taking an anger management test, you will be in a position to see how you react in stressful situations using the method of choice. Also, these tests help you understand how anger affects you as a person and others as well.

You are likely to undergo educationally rooted tests and not for psychiatric or psychological testing. As an individual, you are at liberty of choosing the kind of assessment to undertake, whether an objective or subjective management test, it depends on the intensity or the type of anger you are managing. Still, you don't need to attend a class to undertake the assessment; you can take the test either online or in person.

Taking an anger management test proves to you that if the right measures are applied and practiced, it is possible to manage anger and control emotional outbursts caused by angry feelings. During the test, you will be provided with a questionnaire that gives more insight into the institution of choice on your anger and reactions. While these questions on anger management tests may vary, they attempt to identify emotional and behavioral characteristics individuals with anger management issues may be experiencing. The statements provided give you an answer option, and you will be expected to choose the best answer that applies to you with the consideration that genuineness is key.

The kind of information to be derived from your test will show strengths and weaknesses in various areas;

- Anger expression
- Anger and impulse control
- Ability to manage stressful situations
- Level of aggressiveness towards others
- Level of passiveness
- The skill to communicate feelings and needs
- Acceptance that your anger affects others
- Capacity for change or improvement

This information is important for you as a client but most importantly to the expert handling your program. This is because the answers provided will advise your way forward and give an answer with regards to how bad the situation is or how soft the problem may be. You will eventually come up with an anger control plan as a proactive step to prevent anger. The plan will involve treatment and prevention; however, you will be told that prevention is the best approach. By preventing the anger cycle from even beginning, you are able to stop the actual expression of destructive anger. A well-rehearsed anger control plan will go a long way, but you should put in mind any anger tendencies that have been there before the anger management program and test for the plan to work.

Rehearsing the plan mentally will assist in overcoming the challenge and finding your way out of a situation that may cause anger feelings or even any triggers likely to cause anger. After the test, it is advised that you find ways to unwind and protect yourself from stressors, for example, lack of time, sleep, downtime, exercise, financial pressure, relationship disharmony, among other stressors that contribute to anger.

By undertaking the anger management test, experts will advise if you need to be put through an anger management program or not. You are provided with level measures that tell your movement up and down the anger scale and how fast you are triggered. Depending on the institution of choice, you will see terms like healthy, mild, serious, and extreme, which will then advise the kind of program to enroll in.

Anger management tests are not only important to the victim in this case. It is key that your loved ones or even colleagues partake the test too to assist you in managing anger control difficulties or even pointing out the triggers and origin of the anger. People around you would be able to point out the triggers more than you actually can because they are the secondary subjects, and their judgment is unlikely to be compromised.

10 Anger Management Tips and Strategies

Understanding anger is an important step towards solving your anger issues and difficulties. We are all prone to anger every once in a while. You will realize most individuals are incapable of solving anger difficulties just because people will hardly take their time to understand the anger. Even the simple evaluation of an event brought about by anger proves difficult to most people, therefore, losing the battle to manage anger and rage.

In the case you have evaluated the intensity of your anger, out of the multiple occurrences of angry reactions, it is vital that you come up with tips and strategies for preventing anger outbursts and rage. This may be advised by an anger management test or anger management program. By adapting ways in which you are not prone to anger oriented confrontations and reactions, you stand to benefit a lot in life. Uncontrolled anger will take a toll on your health and your relationships resulting in an unhealthy living style. By taking up strategies and tips for anger management, this does not mean that you will never get angry. In any case, anger is a healthy feeling, but the need to manage it positively is vital.

The best strategies and tips are based on cognitive-behavioral management interventions. These measures involve changing the way you think and behave. The notion behind cognitive-behavioral management is that your thoughts, feelings, and behaviors are intertwined and connected. These strategies help divert negative thoughts or feelings that might fuel your anger. Below are tips and strategies that come a long way in managing anger.

Identify Your Anger Triggers

Anger triggers are actions, deeds, or events that initiate angry emotions in you and are likely to elevate to a response that might cause destruction and damage. Life events impact on how anger triggers choose to surface. They might be deeply rooted in time and previous happenings. Let's say you had a difficult childhood interacting with your peers because they would make a fan of how slender you were, even going ahead to tease you and christen your names. You will be sensitive to what people say about your body once you are an adult, and in a case, a colleague goes ahead to comment on your body shape or frame in the same way, you will be triggered to react and defend yourself.

Taking stock of such simple triggers will give you a deeper insight into the deeper causes of your anger. If traffic triggers your emotions and bars you from normalcy and how you go about your business due to anger, it is also important to note that. You might even come up with simple and destructing activities to indulge in during traffic like reading a book, listening to educative audiobooks, or even applying makeup to pass the time. Whatever circumstance it is that sets you off and prevents you from losing your cool whether alone or around others, identifying it is the first step towards successful anger management.

Learning How to Express Yourself

Most a time when you are angry and full of resentment, you will often blame it on a person or event. This causes more anger considering it is not your 'fault.' By learning to express how you feel about a situation in a calm and collected manner, you are able to let the other party understand where you are coming from and their contribution to your anger and what would have been done or said differently. You are in a position to take your time in between speech and clearly express yourself. This, compared to the obvious outburst that is easy to indulge in than a simple and sober talk goes a long way in solving the situation at hand.

Clearly coming out to express your feelings shows consideration of other parties, but you, this way, you will not hurt others or try to control them. For example, an instance where your fellow colleagues are manipulating a newly employed individual at your workplace by giving the newcomer more work as well as using threatening ways to get him or her to do something, you are at liberty to get angry and confront the situation. However, if you yell at them and expect them to change their behavior, that might cause more trouble and even worsen the situation. By putting your foot down calmly and expressing your concern over the issue, the bad behavior is likely to cease hence a high probability of success.

Taking Time Out

It is advisable that you stop whatever is causing anger feelings and take a deep breath to listen to yourself. Taking time out is not a sign of weakness; in fact, it shows strength while handling a circumstance that might lead to outrage and uncontrollable anger feelings. Whether you decide to chant a mantra, count from one to ten, or even have a series of deep breaths to calm you down during the time out, it is important that you break the process of anger. The few moments of silence and concentration to your thought process will assist in managing your thoughts and feelings.

Practice Relaxation Skills

Different individuals have various ways of relaxing. It is highly advisable that you adopt relaxation skills to suppress any occurring stress that might lead to anger or trigger an unfortunate happening. Anger gives you a rush of energy, and the best solution, in this case, is engaging in physical activity. By moving your body, you highly improve your frustration tolerance. In the event you feel your anger escalating, you can go a brisk walk or run to help relax your mind and have your body moving. You might also indulge in in-house exercise and practice like taking yoga poses to deduce the feeling.

Writing journals on the situation at hand will also encourage relaxation and keep your mind from hosting negative thoughts and feelings likely to fuel anger. These relaxation practices can be chosen according to preference because one method might work for you and fail to provide the same relaxation for someone else.

Seek for Help

Once you set out to manage your anger, it is not an easy process; neither is it a walk in the park. You will be faced with challenges that sometimes might cause you to result from an outburst or even resume previous anger tendencies. Seeking help from a close family member or even friend will assist in evaluating whatever you are going through and how to successfully resume your anger management plan. Also, revisiting an expert does not mean you have lost the battle of fighting uncontrollable emotions of anger, but this could be reinforcing what you already began. As an individual, monitoring your warning signs in order to know when to seek help means that you are true to yourself and therefore motivating you to press on with the change.

Putting Thought into Your Speech

Whenever you need to address an individual or multiple people on a certain issue whether crucial or not, it is important to take your time and put some thought into what you are about to say. For example, if you have been chosen to address family members on an important matter, do not forget each individual comes from a different school of thought and perception is relative. If you happen to trigger any anger feelings or thoughts in them, some of them might choose to reiterate, and in such an event, you will be prone to respond with anger. Also, listening to other parties willing to respond to an issue reduces the chances of saying or doing regrettable things, and the end result will be better understanding and problem-solving.

Focus on the Solution

Instead of dwelling on the issue that has caused your anger, it is advised that you divert your mind and thoughts to the solution. For example, if your child has a habit of putting leftovers in the sink, therefore, forcing you to keep paying the plumber to unblock the pipes, yelling at him or her each time that happens will only cause you more anger that might lead to abusive behavior, finding a solution would be the best move. You might want to train them on how to pour servings for themselves in order to finish the food or buy the child a sizeable bin that suits his height and is also accessible for them. It is key that you keep in mind yelling and calling them names will also have a negative effect on your child.

Invest in Positive Content

Whether it is the kind of music you listen to, books you choose to read, movies, or television shows you invest your time and energy in, it is part of the strategy to acquire positive and helpful content. Content has a way of triggering thoughts and feelings, and it is up to you to make sure it does not send you to a dark place that could trigger anger and behavior that might result in sad feelings. Just like the phrase 'you are what you eat' you are also the content you feed on and choose to consume at any given time. Content has the power to evoke high arousal emotions like joy and fear. Anger is a high-arousal emotion too, and is while consuming content; it might surface unknowingly, therefore, leading to rage.

Realizing Feelings Beneath Your Anger

Anger has been proven to be a reaction used to protect oneself from showing painful emotions such as embarrassment, disappointment, and sadness. Most people lush out without considering the underlying feelings. When someone says something hurtful and demeaning, you might rush for a response in anger to immediately mask the embarrassment it has caused you or even disappointment. By saying it as it is to the subject, and by this, I mean labeling it as it is, you will be in a position to take appropriate action even if it means saying it to the person on the wrong. Just by saying "you really embarrassed me by calling me a hog in front of my children" the person in question will know exactly how you felt about that very happening. But by lashing out and probably banging the door behind you, the individual will know exactly how you feel.

Develop Good Listening Skills

In some instances, anger might be caused by a lack of proper understanding of what was said and why it was said. As part of improving communication, listening gives you a chance to process what you hear, and, in this case, you are able to respond appropriately with a sober point of view. Whether it is a conversation between you and your spouse or with your boss, giving them space to express themselves in between conversation assists in preventing anger or any chance of a misunderstanding. You will be in a position to understand the issue, and even if you have to take time in order to respond, listening plays a big role in controlling feelings of anger.

Anger Management for Kids

Various factors could be contributors to a child's struggle with anger, aggression, or even irritability. Triggering a kid's anger could be as simple as telling them to go to bed early or even finish up homework instead of joining other children in the playing field. Anger in a kid It is highly caused when a child cannot get what he or she wants. It is, therefore, the parent's or guardian's duty to assist manage the child's anger and frustrations that may trigger negative feelings or thoughts such as rage.

Response Modulation

It is not as easy to help a kid understand the intensity of a reaction compared to an adult. Since kids are a lot less predictable with how they respond to frustration and stress, it is key for you to alter psychological, experimental, or even behavioral aspects of a reaction after it has been generated. Since the process of anger is already on, response modulation can help cycle back through the ongoing process. You could anticipate the mishap of a situation and arrest the problem before it turns out to be an overflow of anger feelings. If the child is already upset and the situation is quickly escalating, you could defend the offender as you make your child believe that you root for them, but they have to understand a certain action that happened by accident.

Practicing Anger Management

As an adult, you will need to learn how to control your anger, especially in front of kids to eradicate the vice in them. By solving your own matters when you are come and collected, the child kid will emulate your behavior and eventually, they will adapt unconsciously. In most instances, children assume the 'monkey see monkey do' style of living and therefore look up to the adult when it comes to actions and deeds. Just by being an example, the kid will assume proper anger management as they grow. If you are a vulgar parent who yells at anyone when frustrated or wronged, it is likely that the kid will follow suit and adopt such behavior as they grow older.

Set Ground Rules

Once you realize your child or one your care has difficulties responding to frustration and stress, it is advisable that you sit them down and help them understand in their language that having uncontrollable anger emotions is not right, and it is punishable. For example, when your kid throws tantrums and throws objects across the room or even raising a hand to beat the offender, they should immediately be made aware that it is wrong and not the way to go in such a situation. Make the kid understand how to express themselves without harming others or destroying property.

Since different reactions by kids call for special treatment, monitoring the kid's warning signs and behavior towards stressful situations will assist in prescribing the right measures. Seeking professional help also goes a long way since the kid might listen to an outside voice more than they do at home.

What Is Generalized Anxiety Disorder

Generalized anxiety disorder is persistent and excessive worry about a number of things. If you are suffering from Generalized Anxiety Disorder (GAD), you are likely to anticipate bad happenings that may cause you to overly stress about issues in your life from family, health, work, and even relationships. These worries and concerns are often unfocused and may not necessarily be connected to recent stressful events. You will feel threatened, irritable, restless, and high levels of tension take over your mind and thoughts.

Some of the symptoms that come with the disorder have been said to be solvable only through psychological therapies and medication. Some of the signs may include but not limited to; Overthinking plans and solutions to possibly bad scenarios, Indecisive tendencies to normal situations, a hard time concentrating on an activity or situation, Feeling on edge for no particular reason among other symptoms.

If you are suffering from such, you are likely to withdraw from social contact in order to avoid situations likely to cause worry or dread. Your work routine may be affected since you are likely to ask for multiple sick-offs, and in return, this might cause you to worry even more about what could happen to you or your job, therefore, diminishing self-esteem and belief.

Steps to End Chronic Worrying

Chronic worrying is often diagnosed in people living with Generalized Anxiety Disorder (GAD). If you are a victim of chronic worrying, you worry more than normal people do, and stopping yourself from a spiraling worry and anxiety can be difficult for you. You will realize that chronic worrying is not necessarily rooted in a specific event and one worry births another and most experts will even ask you to stop worrying about worrying. Through self-aid and expert interventions, you could reduce how much you worry by adopting different ways to end chronic worrying.

Practice Positive Self-Talk

Worrying alone is caused or triggered by negative self-talk that then elevates to deep negative thoughts about a situation or person. Once you allow yourself to feed on negative self-talk, you will realize that you start living on a negative edge and expecting bad things to happen all the time. Turning around negative self-talk to positive, you will realize that you will start expecting positive outcomes and occurrences in any given situation. A way to look at it differently would be putting into consideration that whatever it is you would not tell another person is equally not okay for you to tell yourself.

Practice Relaxation Techniques

In order to overcome chronic worry, it is important to stop your thought process and withdraw from your head through relaxation. If it means sitting by the ocean or in a quiet environment and look into the air just to take in the fresh air and beautiful environment, relaxation will calm you down and assist in reducing chronic worry.

Take Control of Your Life

It is easier said than done, especially if you are suffering from chronic worrying. Mostly, a lot of worrying is caused by the feeling of lack of control in your life, either past or future events. Worrying will not solve the issue but taking control of what you are able to manage goes a long way. Life is not a matter of having everything under your control. You cannot control all your life circumstances, but you can choose what you can control and focus on. This way, you will prevent unfocused worries and anxiety.

Forge Relaxation

It might sound vague to ask a victim of chronic worrying to fake relaxation, but psychologically this will work for you. Behaving like you are worried over various things aggravates the situation and causes you to even worry more. Your emotional system assumes calmness and stability if you role-play and stay relaxed therefore assisting you to overcome too much worry.

Acquire Risk Assessment Skills

Anytime you are faced with worry over something that is not a reality on the ground. You should embark on risk assessment and properly evaluate your thought process. Imagine you are in a new relationship, and everything between you and your spouse is running smoothly. Due to the chronic worrying disorder, you will begin worrying about a possible separation, thinking that maybe your spouse will eventually cheat on you or even anticipating a big argument between the two of you. The reality of the matter is that none of this has happened or likely to happen, and therefore reminding yourself of the real situation at hand will stop worrying.

Stress Relief

What Is the Meaning of Stress Relief?

Stress relief is the process and approach of lessening the frustration that situations that might bring about worrying and anxiety that pile up to cause stress. It is conscious control of automatic bodily and mental processes that elevate stress reactions and how you handle them. Since the acquisition of stress is not voluntary, there is a real need for you to exert and influence control over processes such as stress relief. Depending on the intensity or deepness of the stressful situation, you will be needed to explore various ways of stress relief for an impactful end result.

Foods That Can Help Reduce Stress

Stress not only has effects on your mental health but also your physical health. Mostly, strengthening your immunity both mental and physical is key when it comes to stress relief.

An extreme amount of stress will come in the way of your immune, cardiovascular, and central nervous system health and stability. During stress, you are likely to gravitate towards junk food and unhealthy eating habits. However, foods containing the right vitamins, minerals, and foods containing the right vitamins and minerals will help fight stress and hormones likely to fuel stress.

Green leafy vegetables

Leafy vegetables such as spinach contain folate or vitamin B9 that are important in balancing depressive moods. Folate helps produce dopamine in your body system, a brain chemical that helps you stay calm. You tend to be calmer, happier, and energetic once you consume folate.

Oatmeal

Instead of bombarding your body system with unhealthy kinds of carbohydrates, it is advisable that you switch that with oatmeal since it is a complex carb that assists in controlling the glucose in your blood from shooting as opposed to the sugars contained in most carbohydrates.

Salmon

Stress causes anxiety hormones to the spike in your body, with the most common ones being adrenaline and cortisol. Omega 3 fatty acids in salmon counter these hormones and negative effects caused by stress. The acids will protect you from heart problems and disease.

Avocado

Avocados have been proven to counter stress by supplying the body system with vitamin B. Deficiency of the vitamin causes feelings of anxiety. Vitamin B6 provides neurotransmitters that influence your moods as well as heart-healthy fats that increase your immunity.

Cashew Nuts

Cashews provide your body with zinc that assists in reducing the anxiety that in turn dilutes the vulnerability of your body to irritability and the lack of ability to concentrate. Zinc affects the levels of nerve chemical, therefore, allowing better moods, and just like omega-3s, they provide healthy fats for your heart.

Natural Ways of Reducing Stress

Rather than turning to medicine, recreational drugs, or any other self-inflicted substances into your body system, in order to reduce stress, natural ways promise no negative repercussions or even consequences in the long run. Even with the availability of medication that helps reduce stress, doctors often advise that you turn to natural ways if the situation is manageable. Here are some of the natural ways of stress reduction.

Meditation

By slowing down your thought process, you take time out of normal activities or even situations that might spike up your stress levels. Taking a few minutes of mindful therapy allows you to organize your thoughts and eradicate any negative feelings or even anxiety that highly fuels stress levels.

Exercise Routine

You will realize that engaging in physical activity on a daily basis helps decompress and divert your energy to elsewhere as opposed to deep thinking and worrisome behavior. You could sign up for a fitness program or even do it yourself either in the comfort of your home or outdoors to allow unwinding. Exercise will assist in releasing endorphins into the brain hence improving your mood.

Healthy Eating

Taking the right foods improves your well-being and functionality. The release of positive hormones triggered by vitamins and minerals in natural foods reduces your stress levels, and assists in protecting your body from chronic diseases brought about by high levels of stress.

Adequate Sleep

Enough sleep makes the body relax, therefore providing the needed energy for you to go about your day to day activities. Sleep deprivation, on the other hand, leaves you cranky and irritable and this eventually results in high levels of stress. Putting yourself to sleep for the recommended hours rejuvenates your body and system ready to face the next day. Naps too come a long way in putting to rest thoughts that may result in stress.

Taking a Break

In some cases, you will be able to point out your stressor, and this calls for time off from the source of stress. Whether it is your job, relationship, or the environment you are in, stepping away for hours or even days helps reduce stress and gives you time to concentrate on constructive routines of relieving stress.

Ways to Prevent and Relieve Stress

Stress can be inevitable considering we are not in control of most occurrences in our lives. However, it is important that you take the initiative to try and prevent and relieve stress in order to manage your life properly. Stress prevention and relief require you to take charge of your emotions, thoughts and even your environment.

Maintain a Positive Attitude

Although this might seem difficult, intentionally investing in positive thinking and activities keeps the stress away and prevents you from overthinking happenings in your life.

Practice Assertiveness

Your opinions, thoughts, and feelings should be asserted instead of allowing anger to prevail in day to day situations. Being defensive or passive is not healthy for you, and therefore you are prone to high levels of stress.

Make Time for Hobbies and Interests

By dividing your time between work, school, family, and hobbies, you break your routine and familiarize yourself with more than one environment, which highly assists in stress prevention and relief.

Avoid Recreational Drugs

Stress might cause you to turn to recreational drugs like alcohol, bhang, cocaine among other drugs. These drugs only give you temporary relief but leave you stressing even harder and in many a time even stuck at the same point. This is why drowning yourself in such practices gets you even deeper into frustration and in return causing your stress levels to go up.

Choosing to indulge in temporary remedy in order to reduce stress will cause recurring problems that will eventually drive you to depression. Stress is manageable, but only if you have dedicated yourself to a strategy or routine that helps in solving the issue at hand. Since it is a part of everyday life, leaving stress untreated will eventually cost you not only finances and sanity but also relationships in your life.

What is Procrastination?

Procrastination is usually a very active process. It is whereby one decides to attend to other activities instead of purely concentrating on the one task that is due at that exact time. Most people do confuse it with laziness, but it is quite different. Negligence is usually described as an unwillingness to do something or simply being inactive. Procrastination is simply deciding to ignore the most crucial task that is supposed to be done at that moment and decide to do something else that is less important. The reason why people choose the next jobs is that they might be more comfortable and enjoyable to do.

When one gives in to the impulse of procrastinating, you will experience some severe consequences. You can even feel ashamed since you will be able to achieve the set goals you have. Procrastinating for long, demotivate people. Also, they end up being disillusioned with their duties or work. They may later experience depression and lose their jobs as their source of livelihood. Below are the effects of procrastination.

Effects of Procrastination

One is that you will have wasted a lot of your time. Before you realize you have been procrastinating all through. You may have spent five or more years of your life. The years will be quite hard to recover. The feeling is terrible because time is irreversible. The only thing that will happen is that you will leave with guilt and regret. One tends to feel frustrated since you are aware the situation could have been better if only you were cautious.

The second effect is that you will have lost great opportunities. Some opportunities are life-changing ad the best time to work on them is when they arise. You may never be guaranteed another chance, so you do yourself some favor and grab to achieve the best. Thirdly, it will be tough for you to meet your goals. When you are procrastinating, it will be tough for you to take significant steps and move forward to achieve all the goals you have set in place. When you delay, you increase the chances of not making your life better. You need to identify the root cause of the procrastination ad work on it.

Fourth, you may ruin the type of career you have, or you are dreaming of having. The way you do your work affects the results you give at the end. When you procrastinate, you may be unable to beat work deadlines and achieving the set targets. These negative consequences may put a halt to your career or miss out on promotions. It is unnecessary to undermine the work performance you are capable of achieving.

Procrastination is a vicious circle you may find yourself in since it will lower your self-esteem. People procrastinate and make their self-esteem to much lower. With low self-esteem, your confidence will be eaten away slowly by slowly. One ends up feeling less, and you can self-sabotage yourself. Always focus on building your self-esteem.

Lastly, procrastinating damages a person's reputation. Nobody is proud of someone who keeps empty promises. When you keep promising, and you do not fulfill, you get to tarnish your name. These will affect your self-esteem and confidence. You will keep procrastinating since you cannot surprise yourself any other time. Also, people suffer mental problems due to anxiety, stress, and, eventually, depression. Stress and depression are known to be silent killers.

How to Prevent Procrastination

The very first step is to recognize you procrastinate. Always prioritize your tasks, depending on how important they are and how timely they should be complete.

Secondly, know the reason why you procrastinate. Understand the reasons behind it and tackle them very well. You may be avoiding a particular task because of boredom, or it is unpleasant. Strategize on how you will attempt it and have it completed before you move to the enjoyable ones. Ensure you organize yourself so well. When a person is well organized, he or she will prioritize the scheduled tasks so well.

When one adopts excellent strategies to avoid procrastination, you will be in a better position. It is a habit, and that means you cannot easily break it. When you first accept you are procrastinating, one is likely to feel more positive and move on so well. Always get committed to your tasks, focus on completing them on time, and not avoiding them. Tackle tasks as they arise and give no chance for them to build up. In conclusion, ensure when you are working, there are minimal or no distractions at all.

What is Overthinking?

The moment you are overthinking instead of working on things, the right word to describe it is that you are overthinking. Overthinking is the process of analyzing, commenting, and often repeating the same thoughts in your mind again and again without taking a step of action. It ends up wasting your energy and time that you could have used to work on other things that will have your progress in life. When you are overthinking in life, you will always be full of worries, anxiety, and no inner peace at all. It is evident that when one does not overthink, one will be efficient and happy when running daily errands.

Effects of Overthinking

Overthinking causes insomnia. When you have the same thoughts over and over again in your mind, it becomes tough to be relaxed. You are likely not to get enough sleep at night. When laying there on the bed you start to remember similar experiences in the past that instilled pain in you, and you lack sleep. The cycle continues until the next day in the morning. The cycle repeats itself, and you start experiencing mental disorders that are brought about by insomnia, which is chronic.

Another effect is that your life will be very complicated. Have you ever wondered why children have a simple experience? It is because they have not started overthinking. When you overthink, you will not be happy in life. The bottom line is you will think about something over and over again, but without taking action, nothing will change for sure. When you are overthinking, time is also moving.

When you are an over-thinker, you end up being a pessimist, and at the same time, you are unhappy. In the past, people who thought hard were in a better position to make significant decisions. However, recent studies have shown that overthinking may impair the ability to make the decision wisely. One is likely to have irrational thoughts through overthinking. Problems are not solved amicably, and thus, a lot of negativity observed in one's life.

When you overthink, it may lead to depression as well as anxiety. People who overthink are at risk of getting Generalized Anxiety Disorder. Also, they may get attacks caused by panicking and depression. In a situation, it is not right to over analyze, especially if something went wrong. Always look forward to knowing how you can overcome fear, anxiety, and depression in the best manner possible. When depression affects you, the lifestyle you have ends up being affected.

Overthinking makes you have existing or non-existing situations. In such a case, you may not be in control to manage how you approach your thoughts. Whenever you have an issue, you will end up spending a lot of time trying to solve but get no concrete answer. If you over-analyze, you will have the fear that will affect you and as well prevent one from taking the right action. In this, you will lose a lot of opportunities that may need quick responses to acquire success. However, there are solutions to how you can manage to overthink and have the very best happy life.

How to Prevent Overthinking

There are several ways that one can rely on to get rid of overthinking. One can watch their favorite programs on the television. Also, one can do body exercises that will help you get your mind hooked on something else that will have you feeling relaxed. Get anything that will help you stay away from overthinking.

You can also look back and see the amount of time you are consuming when you overthink. It makes you behave passively instead of being an active ad making your life better. You will realize that thinking the same thoughts over and over again is leading one nowhere. One needs to make an informed decision on how you can act well to improve your way of living.

However, to fully overcome the overthinking habit, you need to take another step. Try calming down your mind and purely focus positively, avoiding thinking about issues that are similar to which you got no control. Control the thoughts you have and do not focus on ideas that will lead to restless thinking. Let exercises come in handy.

Chapter 6: How to Be in Control of Your Emotions and Solutions

Can One Control Emotions?

Emotions are feelings composed in your thoughts, and they can be as a result of the situation that you are in or the people around you. It is possible to control your emotions by dealing with them intelligently and staying positive. Some of the emotions include happiness, anger, hatred, love, and fear.

Which Situations May Arouse Emotions?

Some of the situations that can arouse emotions include when you are in a sad or happy situation or when you are scared. The things that surround you or the ones you are thinking about can also arouse emotions. Being in a place where you are treated unfairly or fairly can arouse emotions or being in an uncomfortable situation.

Seven Ways to Control Your Emotions

You need to make sure that you can control your feelings the right way. Here are ways of managing your emotions:

- ***The first thing to do is to select the situation.*** You need to ensure that you get away from conditions that cause unwanted feelings. If you know that there is something that makes you angry or being in a particular situation, you should avoid them. For example, if you get mad when you are late to work, you can always make sure that you wake up early to avoid being late. If being around a particular person makes you frustrated or angry, it is better to avoid that person as much as possible.

- ***Modifying the situation is another way of controlling your emotions.*** You might be feeling disappointed because you cannot do something in the right direction or as you aimed. You can reduce disappointment by finding a good way that you will do that thing the right way or as you expected. For example, you may be willing to prepare a nice meal for your family, but in the end, the meal does not please them. You can avoid the situation by finding a simple recipe on how to prepare that meal and be sure to make a meal that your family will love. In that way, you have modified the situation, and you will not be disappointed.

- ***Shifting your attention and focus is another way of managing your emotions.*** You might be in a situation where you feel inferior because of the people that are surrounding you because they are higher than you. For example, you can be a class group where you are the only one who is less intelligent. They know almost everything, and you keep admiring them and feeling sorry for you.

You can shift your attention to your other classmates you are less intelligent than you. In that way, you will start feeling superior and feel confident about your intelligence. If possible, you can shift from that group and join another one where you will be able to focus on yourself. Through that process, you will start desiring your intelligence, and you won't feel inferior anymore.

- ***Changing your thoughts is another way of controlling your emotions.*** Everyone has beliefs that drive their emotions. One feels sad when something did not work as expected or when they lose a friend. You will also feel happy when something happens as you expected or when you are expecting something good in your life. When you change your thought, you will change how you believe the circumstance is affecting you even when you can't change the situation. For example, to can change your unhappiness thought with some thoughts that bring you joy or happiness.

- ***You can control your emotions by changing your response.*** If you respond to things right away without giving a thought, you may not be able to manage your feelings. You need to regulate your emotions so that you can get control of your response too. For example, when you feel angry or anxious because of something, you should close your eyes and cool yourself down. In that way, you will not have to do anything stupid or be rude to someone. Similarly, if you find that you can't stop laughing in a situation where another person is sad or not smiling, try to force yourself to stop. You might not be able to change your mood but change your facial expression.

- ***You can also control your emotions by labeling them.*** You need to understand the situation that you are in or what you are experiencing before you change your feelings. You need to know if you are feeling sad, disappointed, nervous, or angry and concentrate on what is going on inside you. Number and name all the feelings that you have so that you will have a way of controlling them. It can be hard for you to manage your emotions if you don't know them or what you are going through. Acknowledging your feelings will help you to be careful in the way you react, and you will be able to make the right decisions.

- ***You need to take responsibility for your emotions.*** You are responsible for what you feel when someone makes you angry and how you respond to your emotions. No one can make you feel the way they want if you don't allow them. You can decide to view things in another perceptive such that you will not let them make you angry. You might be expecting someone; they are late, and, in your perception, you don't think it's right, but to them, it is no big deal. In that case, you should take responsibility for your emotions and try to view things positively. Note that people behave in a certain way because of different things such as beliefs, life experiences, culture, and upbringing. That means they can make you angry or happy without them knowing, and it's your responsibility to know how to respond to their actions.

What is Emotional Intelligence?

Emotional intelligence can be defined as the ability to know and control your emotions and emotions of the people around you. It is also the ability to control the emotions and use then in your thinking and solving your problems.

How Can You Improve Emotional Intelligence?

The following are ways that you can increase your emotional intelligence:

- ***You can improve emotional intelligence by using an assertive form of communication.*** When you use assertive communication, you give out your opinion with respect, and others no can annoy you.

- ***You need to respond to conflict instead of reacting.*** When you are in dispute, a feeling of anger will arise, and you need to stay calm about it. You improve the emotional intelligence when you don't react but control your anger.
- ***Make sure that you use active listening skills when you are in a conversation with another person.*** You improve your emotional intelligence when you listen carefully and understand before you respond. In that way, there will be no misunderstanding, and it shows that you have respect for the other person.
- ***You also increase your emotional intelligence when you stay motivated at all times.*** You should be self-motivated and have an attitude that excites you. In that way, you will not have to deal with feelings such as sadness and disappointments.
- ***You can also improve emotional intelligence by having positive attitudes.*** A negative attitude is dangerous, and you can even infect others. In that case, ensure that you have a way of having a positive attitude every day. Do things that make you optimistic.
- ***You improve your emotional intelligence by practicing self-awareness.*** It is best to be aware of your emotions and how they can affect the people that are around you.
- ***Be friendly and approachable too.*** That means that you need to use the right social skills according to the relationship you have with those around you. Show a positive presence such that people can approach you when they a problem.
- ***You can also improve your emotional intelligence by empathizing with other people.*** Showing empathy is a sign of emotional strength and not a weakness.

How Is It Applicable to Helping You Deal with Emotions?

Emotional intelligence is applicable in the following areas:

- Emotional intelligence can be applied when you are in an argument or a conversation with the other person. It helps you to listen carefully before giving your response.
- You can use emotional intelligence when you are angry, and instead of expressing your feelings to others, you calm yourself down.
- You can also use emotional intelligence when you conflict. It will help you respond to it instead of reacting.
- When you have problems instead of overthinking, you use emotional intelligence to solve your problems.
- You can apply it when you make a mistake and accept you did it and apologize
- Having emotional intelligence can help you to forget a lousy moment easily and be able to move on.
- You can use emotional intelligence to get along with different people and situations
- It can be applied to change criticism to a constructive one without blaming the other people.

How to Deal with Emotions Healthily?

When it comes to your emotions, you need to ensure that you deal with them the right way without affecting the people around you. For you to deal with your feelings healthily, you need to understand that emotions are natural. That means expressing them is healthy, but you need a way of showing them the right direction. Adjusting your expectations is another way of dealing with your emotions healthily. You might feel frustrated or disappointed because you expect too much from others or yourself. For example, if you are a mother, you should not follow what others tell you to be a perfect mum, but you should be realistic.

Don't try to be perfect, but be a good mother as you can. Learning how to accept how things or people are a healthy way of dealing with your emotions. For example, if you don't like how your kid behaves, you need to accept that way. Instead of shouting at him, you can find the right way of communicating with him.

However, if it is hard for you to deal with your emotions by yourself, you can seek help from psychologists. They will help you to understand your feelings quickly and how to deal with them healthily.

What Are the Effects of Negative Emotions?

Having a negative emotion has many effects, especially on your health and people that surround you. Having a negative emotion can lead to health problems such as chronic stress. It can lead to a more serious health problem that shortens your life spun. Having a negative emotion can make you aggressive, and it will be hard for you to live with other people in peace. You will find that you are always angry and rude because you have a negative emotion. It will be impossible for you to be happy when you have a negative feeling, and most of the time, you will be sad. Negative emotion also makes you feel demotivated and underestimating your capabilities. When you have such emotions, it is hard for you to reach your goals because you think it is a hard thing for you. Another effect of negative emotion is poor decision making. When you are not thinking positively, you can hardly make the right decision, and it is hard to solve your problems.

There are other effects of negative emotion in your health, such as high blood pressure, digestive disorders, infection, and cardiovascular disease. You can avoid such health problems by making sure that you maintain a positive emotion always. With a negative emotion, you will find that you can deal with critics, and instead, you react by fighting and yelling at others. That will make your relationships with others to break, and you may find yourself alone without any friends.

Conclusion

Thanks for making it through this book. Let's hope it has provided all the necessary information that you were looking for. You have successfully gained substantial information concerning various emotions, and you have reflected on your emotions. Though the book provided comprehensive coverage on the topic you can go ahead and do more research on the same to expand your knowledge base further.

Since you are done with the book, you can go ahead and share the information with your friends, teach them what you have learned while at the same time you try putting into practice what you have learned. Build yourself positively, and since you are knowledgeable on the subject matter be ready to help those victims who succumb to negative emotions as you have learned.

The book has crossed borders to bring any relevant information. You too, should cross the border and make this information useful. If you were at a crossroads and didn't know anything about emotions help somebody else by assisting them to see the light out of depression, anger, and fear by sharing this vital book.

If this book provided helpful information, or along the way you noticed something helpful, kindly share it and assist somebody in finding a solution to emotional-related problems.